How under the blue moon do you think of all this crazy stuff?

    —Rosa

Keep writing! I love it!

    —Sean

Love your book!

    —Benjamin

I love your hilarious stories!

    —Ivy

I think you're really funny, and I really enjoy reading your stories. Where can I buy your book? Keep doing what you're doing.

    —Sarah

I am a big fan of yours and love your funny adventures! Keep up the good work! I don't have your book yet, but I read *Clubhouse* magazine and love your stories. :) Especially the one where it snowed there in Texas. What was your latest adventure? I know you are always getting into some adventure! Thank you for the wonderful stories.

    —Caitlyn

I love you, Average Boy!

    —Charlie

I'm a huge fan of yours! Your blogs are really funny.

    —Crystal

Hi, Bob! I *love* your stories. You're really funny. You remind me so much of my younger brother (he's nine).

    —Ellie

I love your stories.

—BLAZE

You rock.

—EMMY

You're my friend (even though I have never met you).

—JEREMY

I am a new fan of Average Boy. Your stories are so funny.

—REBEKAH

Every time I get the magazine, I go to your page first!

—HANNAH

You are hilarious!

—CODY

Just wanted to say I ♥ your stuff!

—GIGI

Just started reading [Average Boy], and I think you're hilarious.

—RACHEL

I read your stories to my mom, and she *loves* them!

—REBECCA

I love your stories. You couldn't possibly make them funnier!

—ANNA

Thanks so much for being so funny! Reading your stories really cheers me up.

—SARAH

DEVOTIONS FOR

SUPER AVERAGE KIDS

30 Adventures With God For Kids Who Like to Laugh

by Bob Smiley and Jesse Florea

BOOK

2

Tyndale House Publishers, Inc., Carol Stream, Illinois

I would first like to dedicate this book to the guy who invented books. Without him this probably wouldn't have been possible. I also wish to thank Wendy (who I've had a crush on forever) and Colter, Trent, and Zander—my own little super average boys! Now let's start some more adventures!

—BOB

For Arianna, Katie, Owen, and every child who's on the awesome adventure of following God. Forget about average. Be super average!

—JESSE

Contents

Meet Average Boy—Again

Name: Bob Smiley

Middle Name: Something worse than Gertrude

Height: Five feet eight inches . . . unless my mom makes me comb down my hair

Weight: 118 pounds, while holding my dog; otherwise I'm 98 pounds.

Hometown: Leo, Texas

Favorite Breakfast Cereal: Frosted Sugar Barrel Bombs with one layer of granola sprinkled on top to make it healthy

Best Friend: Billy the Great and Amazing, who always reads this part of the book

Favorite Animal: My dog . . . for weight and companionship purposes

Longest Time Spent Riding That Animal: Nine seconds (would've been longer had that tree branch not been hanging down so low)

Favorite Book of the Bible: James

Favorite Olympic Sport: Standing on the gold medal winner's pedestal

Favorite Subject in School: English, becauze I'm really very well at it

Daily Routine: Wake up. Have a crazy adventure. Come home and write about it.

Greatest Accomplishment: Telling people about Jesus

Favorite Bible Verse: Joshua 1:9

Favorite Hero from the Bible: Jesus (Anyone who will die for me is the kind of hero I want!)

Favorite Memory: That time I went to that place . . . *hmmm.* I can't really remember what it's called.

Least Favorite Memory: When Billy's fence fell down. I still say the slingshot bike will work one day!

The Skinny on Bullying

i became a hero today! Come to think of it, I'm an unsung hero because nobody's written a song about me. Maybe you will after you read this chapter.

I've always been skinny. I know this because I have a mirror. But in case I ever forget, kids remind me of this fact all the time . . .

"You're so skinny that you can use ChapStick as deodorant."

"You're so skinny that if you put a dime on your head, people would think you're a nail."

"You're so skinny that your pants only have one belt loop."

"You're so skinny that you could hula-hoop with a Cheerio."

I hear stuff like that all the time. But Kyler's so skinny that he can dodge raindrops.

Once Kyler told me he used venetian blinds as a bunk bed. He's fine with the fact that God made him skinny, but some kids at school pick on him. Today was no exception.

It started with Clint and Clay standing by their lockers (insert bad-guy music here). Kyler and I walked up to grab our books for the next class (now switch to hero music).

"Did someone order two Popsicle sticks?" Clay joked.

Kyler ignored him and swung open his locker door just as Clint jumped toward me to start the flinching game.

Do you know this game? A big kid acts like he's going to punch you. Then you flinch because it's encoded in your DNA to avoid bodily harm. That's followed by the big kid saying the only words in the game: "Two for flinching." Then he hits you two times in the arm. I don't know who invented this game, but it wasn't a skinny kid.

Anyway, Clint jumped at me headfirst. This would've been a nice move in the flinching game had Kyler's locker door not swung open and hit Clint right in the face.

Clang!

"Awww, my nose!" Clint said, holding his face.

"Yeah, maybe you should *nose* better than to pick on other kids," Kyler said.

It was a funny line, but not the smartest one to say. Fortunately, Mr. Gribble, our janitor, walked around the corner at that exact moment.

"You boys get to class," he said.

Clint turned to Kyler and mouthed the words, "Poor Fred."

As it turned out, I'm bad at lipreading. What Clint actually mouthed was "You're dead."

For the next three hours, news spread all over school that Clint was going to beat up Kyler in the locker room after gym class. I know gossip is bad, but this time it helped. It gave me time to make a plan. I began passing notes to all the skinny kids. I didn't know if they'd help, but I had to try.

Gym class finally came. We played sock ball, which used to be called dodgeball before lawyers made teachers exchange the balls for socks. All through the game I could tell Kyler was nervous about what was waiting for him in the locker room.

Sure enough, when Kyler walked in, Clint and Clay were already there. Kyler tried to go to his locker, but Clint cut him off.

"Look," Kyler said. "It was an accident. I just want to change and go to my class."

"Not till you pay," Clay said.

That's when I heard the first towel go *pop*!

I knew right then that my plan was going to work. I looked around the locker room and saw 19 skinny kids with towels wrapped and ready to snap.

Did You Know?

- Thousands of children miss school at least one day every month because they're afraid of being bullied.
- In 2011, almost seven million students between 12 and 18 years of age said they'd been bullied during the school year.
- Bullies often travel in packs, preying on the weak and injured.*

*Oh wait, that's wolves. But it's also true about bullies, who usually smell like wolves. By the way, if you're wondering where I found all the interesting facts and statistics I talk about in this book, see the "Data Bank of Facts" section in the back.

"You may be able to beat us all up," Glasses McQueen said, stepping forward. "But you aren't getting out of here without a ton of welts from our towels. There's more of us than there are of you."

I quickly did the math, and Glasses was right! Clint looked around the locker room at a bunch of towel-wielding, skinny kids who were tired of getting picked on. And he left! He just turned and ran. Clay stood there, but not for long.

"Hey, this isn't my fight," he said. "I'm outta here."

Afterward, Kyler thanked Glasses. Glasses told him to thank me, because I'd written a note to everybody mapping out a plan to stand up to these bullies once and for all. Hopefully just once.

So that's how I became a hero. Let the song writing begin!

Super Average Advice

Bullying can become a vicious cycle, which sounds like a bike with sharp teeth and claws. But it's not. A vicious cycle is when one trouble leads to another one that stirs up the first trouble again. Pretty soon the problem spins around and around in a circle, getting totally out of control.

Nobody likes to be bullied. Many kids who experience bullying want to seek revenge. But revenge is like building a bridge over a deep canyon. You should leave it to the experts.

The only expert in revenge is God. Romans 12:19 says, "Friends, do not avenge yourselves; instead, leave room for His wrath. For it is written: Vengeance belongs to Me; I will repay, says the Lord."

Gathering a bunch of friends to stand up to a bully may work, but it's not always a good idea. It may escalate the situation, causing additional conflict and pain.

At the same time, doing nothing to stop a bully is like wearing muddy boots in a bathtub. You'll end up standing in a muddy puddle. (Hey, that sounds funny. Try saying "muddy puddle" 10 times fast.) Wait, a muddy puddle?

Yes, the Bible says, "Like a muddied spring or a polluted fountain is a righteous man who gives way before the wicked" (Proverbs 25:26, ESV). As followers of Christ, we should stand up to evil. And experts say the best way to stop bullying is to get an adult involved.

If you see or experience any bullying, tell an adult you trust—a parent, a teacher, a coach, your principal. And don't forget to pray. God will give you the courage, strength, and wisdom to stand up to bullying in the best possible way. When you share what's happening with an adult, you're not being a tattletale. You're being a hero . . . even if you never get a song written about you.

God's Guide

Read: Ecclesiastes 4:9–10, 12

1. Why is it often better to work together instead of by yourself?
   More work done. help

2. These Bible verses can relate to many areas of life—friendship, helping each other, even marriage. How do you think they relate to bullying?

You stick up for each other

BONUS ACTIVITY

Want to be great at dodgeba—er, sock ball? First, never stand still. Keep on your toes and keep moving. Second, when you want to get someone out, fake a low throw at his feet. If he jumps, throw hard at him in the air when he's not able to move.

2

Dial R for Responsibility

Last month my parents broke down and bought me a phone! I don't mean they finally gave in to my begging. Our car actually broke down right in front of a cell-phone store. God's timing is perfect!

"God is telling us I need a cell phone," I said.

"I think He's saying we need a new car," Dad replied.

We have the cheapest, smallest car in the world. The only good thing about it is that parking is easy. My dad just picks it up and puts it where he wants. Or he carries it around in his pocket.

Okay, it's not that small. But when I first saw it, I thought Dad had bought a riding lawn mower. I got down on the ground, looked underneath, and said, "They forgot to put the blade under here."

My dad didn't laugh.

Dad loves to tell how he and Mom chose the car. Mom said she wanted something that would go from zero to 150 in three seconds. So Dad bought her a scale. He tells this joke a lot, despite the bruising from where my mom hits his arm.

The car they settled on could go from zero to 60 . . . sometimes. It's not fast, but it did come with the one feature Dad wanted: He could afford it.

Anyway, earlier as we were riding in the car, I passed the time by watching things pass us. Things like cars, an elderly lady using a walker, and a feather caught in the wind. All of a sudden, the car started shaking like crazy! My brother and I thought it was fun because we kept bashing into each other in the backseat.

Then the car jerked forward very hard and died. This was awkward mostly because my brother and I were thrown into the front seat with my parents. (Did I mention the seat belts weren't very good either?)

My dad reached into his pocket for his phone, which wasn't there. He'd left it at home. Well, someone did. He claims I was

Did You Know?

- The Peel P50—which weighs 130 pounds—holds the Guinness World Record as the smallest car ever mass-produced. Handmade in Great Britain, this one-seater's speed tops out at 30 miles per hour.
- The legal driving age in Alberta, Canada, is 14.
- The Bugatti Veyron Super Sport car boasts the highest sticker price of any street-legal production automobile. The base model costs $1.7 million, but add some options, and the price soars to $2.4 million. The car does, however, go from zero to 60 in 2.5 seconds. (If you're considering this for my birthday, I like the blue one.)

playing a game on it before we left. Thankfully I proved him wrong once we got home.

"See, your phone is right here where *you* left it . . . uh . . . lying on my bed." Okay, so maybe it was my fault. The point is, we didn't have a phone.

"Maybe I can fix it," Dad said. We all had a good laugh at that until his look told us he wasn't joking.

Dad popped the trunk to get his tools. That's when I knew his day wasn't going to improve. The day before, I'd taken out his tools to fix my bike. My bike has an annoying way of coming apart any time I crash it into a tree, which happens a lot. Well, I'd forgotten to put the tools back in the truck.

"WHERE ARE MY TOOLS?" Dad asked quietly enough that people in Oklahoma might not have heard him.

"Probably at home using your phone?" I tried.

"No phone! No tools! You see why I tell you to put things back?" Dad asked.

"Maybe the cell-phone store has a phone," my brother piped in.

We walked over to the store, and sure enough it had a phone. Six hundred of them. That's when God stepped in! Instead of finding a phone, we found a mechanic shopping for a phone to buy for his son. He said he wanted his son to have a phone in case of emergencies, and everything was on sale today.

"No one has more emergencies than me," I said.

Dad didn't reply.

Anyway, the mechanic found the problem. The car had overheated.

"How? I told Bob to put radiator fluid in the car three days ago," Dad said.

"Oh yeah." I smiled. "Let me do that now while the hood is up."

No one laughed . . . again.

"I'm sorry," I said, hanging my head. "I left your phone, took the tools out of the car, and forgot to put in radiator fluid. It's my fault. I guess I'm not that responsible."

"I like when you own up to your responsibilities," Dad said. "And you know what? Maybe you do need a phone for emergencies. Let's go look at those bargains."

An hour later our car was full of radiator fluid, and we were flying down the highway at a brisk 34 miles an hour!

"I see why you want us to put things back and do our chores right away," I said to my parents. "I promise to get better at that."

And I meant it. I wasn't just saying that because they got me a phone. Now I just had to figure out how to ask them to turn around. I left my new phone at the store.

Super Average Advice

Spider-Man's Uncle Ben said it best, "Peter Parker, stop climbing those walls. You're getting web everywhere!"

Oh wait, that's not the right quote. But he did tell his nephew, "With great power comes great responsibility."

Right now you probably feel like adults have all the fun and power. They get to drive. They don't have to go to school. They can eat double-fudge, chocolate-chip ice cream whenever they want. They can tell their kids what to do. They have a bunch of bills to pay. They work a lot. They get to vote.

Okay, being an adult is not all fun. There is a downside. One of the drawbacks is all the additional responsibilities . . . not to mention their nose hair grows at an alarming rate.

You're probably responsible to keep your room clean, take care of your pets, and do well in school. Your parents have those same responsibilities (except they need to excel at work, not school), plus 50 more. When they give you a job to do, they're training you to be successful in the future.

As you grow, you'll want more freedom and power, like having a cell phone or driving a car. But the web-slinger's uncle was right: With power (and freedom) comes responsibility. Prove you're responsible by following these tips:

Be faithful in the little things. We all want to be in charge of something important. But before somebody can become president and run a country, he has to prove his leadership by successfully running an organization or a state. And before some parents let their children get a dog, the kids have to prove they can be responsible by taking care of a fish or a gerbil. (Just make sure not to try and walk your fish.)

Jesus put it this way: "One who is faithful in a very little is also faithful in much, and one who is dishonest in a very little is also dishonest in much" (Luke 16:10, ESV). So if you're asked to do something little, like putting back the tools after you use them, make sure you do it.

Think of others. One of the best ways to build responsibility is to think of how your actions affect those around you. If you don't walk the dog, who loses? If you fail to finish your chores, who has to pick up the slack? When you follow through on your responsibilities, you make life better for everyone—including yourself.

God's Guide

Read: Colossians 3:23–24

1. When you show responsibility, who's pleased with your actions? List everybody you can think of.

   The Lord
   yourself
   mom

2. Write down some areas where you can show more responsibility. What do you hope to gain by proving you can be responsible?

   your room

BONUS ACTIVITY

Put on a long-sleeved shirt and tape two cans of Silly String around your wrists. Then leap out when your parents are watching TV, say, "My Spidey sense is tingling," and start shooting out a fun "web." (It's okay to take full credit for this awesome idea. In fact, *don't* tell your parents where you heard this.)

The Game of Life

I'm moving out!"

"That's fine," Dad said. "I've already got most of your money."

If our neighbors were listening, they might have thought there was disharmony in the Smiley home. But just the opposite was true. Tonight is Family Game Night, and my player was finally able to move out of my dad's hotel.

Most Friday nights we play a board game called Your Life. It's a very realistic game where we all end up millionaires.

We've had this game so long that we've lost most of the pieces. The game came with five small plastic people that moved around the board. Somehow they've all mysteriously disappeared. Actually, my dog ate two of them. So technically they disappeared and then reappeared. But nobody wanted to use them anymore.

And I know what happened to the fifth person. Our family only has four members, so we never used the yellow plastic person. One night I leaned him against a candle so he could watch his other friends play. Bad idea. By the time the game was over, he had turned into a plastic puddle.

So now we bring our own characters to the game. Seeing what everybody brings actually adds to the fun.

Tonight I was an arm from one of my broken action figures. My dad chose a hard-boiled egg. My brother was a potato chip. But when he got up to get a drink, I . . . er, I mean, someone ate him. He's now a saltshaker. My mom forgot to bring something, so she's the yellow plastic puddle guy.

Anyway, I had just moved off my dad's hotel. I paused, thinking of what to do next. This game takes a lot of skill. And by "skill" I mean you have to be able to pick up and read a card.

Of course, reading the cards can be a challenge. We lost the original cards. They disappeared a little at a time until we finally got down to just five cards. This made the game predictable, so my dad came up with a great idea to make new cards. He handed out square pieces of paper and told us to write down anything we could remember from the old cards.

Well, either our memories are really bad or we all saw an opportunity for a good prank. I was the first one to draw a new homemade card, and I'm pretty sure "Bark like a dog at a passing car" was not in the original deck.

I looked at my brother and said, "Nice try, but I'm not barking like a dog."

"It has to be at a car," my mom pointed out. "That's what my . . . uh, the card said."

That was just the beginning. My dad made lots of cards with

chores on them. He said he thought it'd be funny. I have to admit that I did laugh when he drew the "Mow lawn" card.

Eventually we got rid of the prank cards. When it was my turn again, I drew a card with my brother's handwriting on it that said, "Move ahead to the next player's square. Knock that person back to Start." I looked up to see Dad's hard-boiled egg six squares in front of me.

"Not only am I past your hotel," I shouted, "I'm knocking you back to Start!"

Now two things could've been done to prevent what was about to happen:

1. My brother could've used a better word than *knock*.

2. Dad could've listened better about which carton had hard-boiled eggs and which carton had regular eggs.

I took my action figure arm and knocked my dad's egg back

Did You Know?

- Monopoly is the world's best-selling board game. Translated into more than 40 languages and available in over 110 countries, it's sold more than 275 million games, which have included over six billion little green houses.
- Board games can help kids with shape recognition—can anyone say Candy Land?—as well as social skills like communicating, sharing, and taking turns.
- In the game Sorry!, it's okay if you don't feel sorry about knocking someone's piece back to Start.

toward the starting space. I heard a huge crack and watched as yellow goop poured onto the board. I froze, expecting my dad to get mad.

Sure enough, his voice filled the room . . . with laughter. Then he tilted the board forward.

"I win," he said. "My yolk made it to the finish line before the puddle, the shaker, and your arm-*y*!"

If your family doesn't have a family game night, I suggest you start one. I'm even willing to sell our version of Your Life . . . if you aren't allergic to eggs.

Super Average Advice

What does your family do for fun?

In some families, everybody has different interests. It's okay if you're a sports fan, your sister likes cats, your brother's into cars, your dad's a musician, and your mom juggles chain saws. (Well, except for maybe the cats—those things can be dangerous.) But in spite of different interests, all families need to find activities that bring everybody together.

For some families, that's bike riding, stamp collecting, or preparing a meal and eating together. Other families look forward to watching a favorite TV show every week or (*hint, hint*) reading a book together! Family game nights can be awesome as well.

No matter what you do, spending time with family is important. God wants your family to be close. Even if you have challenges or disagreements, God put you in your family for a reason. Work at

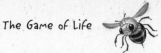

your relationships with your parents and siblings to make them as strong as they can be.

When you have a firm foundation in your earthly family, it reflects God's family. Think about this: There's God the Father and Jesus the Son, and we—who believe in Him—are His children. That's a tight family! And God wants our earthly families to be just as close.

Take a few minutes to write down some things you'd like to do with your family for fun:

1. _____

2. _____

3. _____

Show your ideas to a parent and make plans to do something on your list. Maybe a different family member could choose an activity each week to do together.

Not only does God want us to have strong families so we can feel loved and accepted, but He also uses our families to teach us about Him. Proverbs 1:8 says, "Listen, my son, to your father's instruction, and don't reject your mother's teaching."

Part of a parent's job is to give you instruction and advice—not to mention love and cookies. You need to listen to what your parents say and honor them with your actions.

And when you totally beat your parents in a game of Sorry!, just remember that God gave you a family to help you through the real game of life.

God's Guide

Read: Ephesians 6:1–4

1. What are some benefits of obeying your mother and father?

   _____

   _____

2. Do you ever get angry at your parents? What do you do when you're mad at them?

   _____

   _____

   _____

3. Why is it important to have a strong relationship with your parents?

   _____

   _____

BONUS ACTIVITY

Create a new board game with your family by combining two already existing ones. For example, you could mix Angry Birds and Twister to make Angry Twister.

Foul-Mouthed Singers

Clint and Clay must have grown up sailing, because they cuss like sailors. Isn't that a funny phrase, "cusses like a sailor"? I wonder who came up with that, since we never hear such phrases as "sews like a tailor," "delivers like a mailer," or "harpoons like a whaler." Those seem to make a lot more sense.

Anyway, my grandfather put it best: "When people use swearwords, they show a lack of a good vocabulary."

Of course, later that day he hit his thumb with a hammer and proved he needed to study his vocabulary words a bit more too. So for Christmas that year, I bought him a dictionary!

I started thinking about swearwords the other day in music class. As we practiced our songs for the recital, my teacher called me to the front of the class.

"I'd like to move you into the back row of the choir," she said. "Try not to sing so loudly."

"Is it so the other kids won't feel bad, because they'll realize they can't sing as well as me?" I whispered to her.

"Uh, yeah," she whispered back. "Let's go with that."

So I moved to the back of the room next to Clint and Clay. When we started the first song, I noticed Clint and Clay had made up their own version. Any word that rhymed with a swearword was taken out—and a swearword was put in its place. They sang low enough that no one in the front could hear.

I guessed they were cussing because they thought it was cool—which it's not. First, it doesn't honor God. Second, it's offensive.

Once I was sitting at a baseball game with my dad. The guy sitting next to us wasn't happy with the umpire, and he had no problem expressing his feelings. People around him were getting very uncomfortable. Plus, there were a lot of kids around.

"Uh, sir," my dad finally said, "could you stop cussing in front of all these kids?"

"I'm not cussing in front of all the kids," the guy said. "I'm cussing behind that one up there."

That's when that kid's dad turned around and gave him a look.

"You're right," the guy added. "Sorry, I just get so mad at my brother when he calls a strike when it's obviously a ball!"

Clint and Clay didn't seem sorry at all. They kept smiling and laughing as they threw cusswords into all the songs. When class finished, Clint asked me what I thought.

Putting on my most sophisticated accent, I tried to pass along what my grandfather said to me: "The problem is you're too assiduous when dealing with inferior or illicit words in order to produce wrathful feelings from others around you. I suggest you absolve those wrongdoings and exonerate those amongst us all."

Wow, Grandpa was right! You do sound a lot smarter when you don't use cusswords. I'll have to thank him for letting me read his dictionary when his TV broke last Christmas.

Clint didn't seem as impressed. He stared blankly and said, "Say what?"

"What," I said, laughing. "Look, I know you guys think cussing is funny, but it's just a lack of a good vocabulary. It's not funny. It's actually kind of sad."

This is normally the part of the story where I tell you how things turned out great. I'd like to write that Clint and Clay agreed to stop cussing forever. But this is real life. This isn't some movie or book. Uh, actually this is a book. But Clint and Clay didn't listen to me. They told me to shut up and continued to throw cusswords into the songs.

The next day I came up with a plan. I secretly convinced the rest of the class to stop singing during one of the songs. This left Clay and Clint singing a duet. Without the rest of our voices, their new lyrics carried up to the front of the room and into our teacher's ears.

Did You Know?

- Experts say that children begin swearing as early as age two, and by the time they start school, they know around 30 or 40 bad words.
- Some words can have bad meanings in countries outside the United States, so it's important to watch what you say.
- If somebody calls you a "little cuss," that's not necessarily a bad thing. It's just an old-fashioned way of saying "fellow."

She and the principal quickly put an end to song parodies.

Now if you will excuse me, I need to go get the dictionary. My grandfather just started repairing our fence.

Super Average Advice

You can do a lot of cool things with your mouth. You can sing, speak, eat, spit, hum, and smile. And if you're really talented, you can do all of those things at once.

A lot of kids think it's cool to cuss with their mouths. Maybe they think it makes them appear older, tougher, or edgy. Or perhaps they're practicing for a career in rap music.

You probably hear plenty of bad words around school, in movies, at parks, and anywhere else you hang out. You may even be tempted to use that kind of language yourself. Hanging around friends who have nasty vocabularies makes it more difficult to keep your own speech pure.

Don't forget that God wants us to keep our words and our lives holy. In Matthew 15:10–11, Jesus told a crowd, "Listen and understand: It's not what goes into the mouth that defiles a man, but what comes out of the mouth, this defiles a man."

Your speech and actions should set you apart. Instead of blending into the crowd with the way you talk, you should stand out. Your words reflect your heart. If you tell gross jokes to get a laugh, or if you spew hurtful words, you're not using your mouth in the way God intended.

But taming the tongue takes terrific toughness (try saying that five times fast). Turning to God's Word can help. A great verse for you to memorize is Ephesians 5:4 (NIrV): "There must not be any unclean speech or foolish talk or dirty jokes. All of them are out of place. Instead, you should give thanks." Write that verse on a note card and tape it on your bathroom mirror where you'll see it every day. Keep reading that verse every time you brush your teeth until you can say it without looking. Then strive to live up to that high standard with your speech.

And although you can't control what your classmates say, you can explain to your friends that you'd prefer they not swear around you. Tell them you're trying to clean up what comes out of your mouth. Maybe your stand will encourage others to quit cussing too. Remember to pray and ask God to give you strength to be a light for Him with your speech . . . and with everything else that comes out of your mouth.

God's Guide

Read: Ephesians 4:29

1. Foul language goes beyond cussing. It includes put-downs, angry talk, cruel teasing, and name calling. Why do you think God wants no foul language to come out of your mouth?

    _____

    _____

    _____

    _____

2. How can you build people up with your speech? Write down some specific ways you can give grace to others with your words.

_____

_____

_____

_____

BONUS ACTIVITY

Make up a version of "Twinkle, Twinkle, Little Star" with new funny words and then sing it for your family.

Lifestyles of the Rich and Ignored

Richie Woodward's parents have a lot of money. I think that's why they named their child Richie.

Richie comes to school with a new lunch box every week. He always has the coolest shoes, the best backpack, and the fastest bike. So when he invited me to spend the night, I couldn't wait. I wanted to see how rich people lived.

My dad dropped me off at Richie's house. Actually, we drove past it first because we thought it was a mall. But we checked the address and circled around. My dad knows Richie's dad pretty well. They play golf together once a month.

"I like playing golf with Mr. Woodward because he's funny, and he always pays for everything," my dad said.

I knocked on the huge door and waited . . . and waited. My dad rolled down his car window and told me to use the doorbell.

"Maybe they're in the food court and can't hear you!" he joked.

So I walked over and pressed a glowing button. The door

opened a few minutes later. My dad waved and drove off. I looked at Mr. Woodward. He was wearing a suit and white gloves. I started to introduce myself, but he interrupted.

"You are Master Richie's friend here to spend the night."

Master? So Richie was his middle name. I don't blame him for going by Richie. I wouldn't want people calling me Master all the time.

"Nice white gloves," I replied. "Did you just get home from your job as a mime?"

He didn't laugh. He just looked at me and said, "Mmmm. Yes, Master Richie told me you were funny."

Thankfully, Richie showed up at the door.

"Hey! I see you met our butler," he said. "Come on in."

Butler! I thought. *That makes sense, because he didn't seem funny at all.*

I walked inside and saw a huge wide-screen TV and several couches. It was the biggest living room ever.

"This room is awesome!" I said.

"Thanks," Richie said. "You should see our living room. That's where the big TV is."

Turns out I was in the sitting room—not the living room. I had no idea there were entire rooms for sitting! I'd been sitting in whatever room I felt like.

The rest of their house was even more amazing. Their faucets poured out hot water right away! That might not sound too impressive, but at my house, you never know when the hot water might show up or how long it will last.

Richie's room was like my room . . . if my room was a sporting-goods store. Half of his room looked like a gym floor with a basketball hoop on the wall. I quickly took a shot and missed by three feet, so I knew the goal was set at the proper height. He also had three video-game systems, and his bed looked like a spaceship!

"Richie, this place is amazing!" I said as I picked up some darts to throw at his dartboard. "You've got the best life."

"Not really," he replied.

Shocked, I quickly turned. I then made a mental note to remember to never turn when throwing a dart.

"Oops, that dart was a little off target," I said. "Sorry."

"That's okay," he said. "I didn't like that wall clock anyway."

"But why don't you think you have an amazing life?" I asked. "You have everything!"

"My parents ignore me," Richie said. "They buy me stuff, thinking it makes me happy. But my mom spends all her time at the

Did You Know?

- In January 2013, C Seed Entertainment unveiled a TV with a 201-inch screen! Priced at over $600,000 and rising to a height of 15 feet, the TV can be folded up to store and is too big to fit in most houses.
- If you have food in a refrigerator, clothes in your closet, and a bed to sleep in, you are richer than most of the world's population.
- The average home size in the 1950s was almost 1,000 square feet. Today, that's the size of some people's three-car garages.

country club or shopping. My dad plays golf every day instead of coming home. We never eat dinner together."

"Oh, but what about your butler?"

"That's not the same," he said. "Your dad is always playing baseball with us. You guys camp and fish together. You've got the best life."

I had to admit he was right. I may not have the coolest clothes or a spaceship for a bed. But I have parents who love me. The Bible says money can't buy happiness. Richie had it all, but he wasn't happy.

The next Saturday my dad and Mr. Woodward had a golf date. As they teed off on the first hole, Richie and I walked up.

You see, I'd told Richie that his parents might not realize he wanted to spend time with them, so we decided to crash this golf game.

We all had a blast hanging out together. Actually, my dad didn't start having fun until I told him that Richie paid for my round of golf. And at the end, Mr. Woodward said he wanted to do more stuff with Richie!

That night I thanked God for my parents and for the reminder that love is more important than money. Then I started sketching out plans for my new spaceship bed!

Super Average Advice

Bigger is better. The latest is the greatest. Too much is never enough.

Do you agree with those statements? Many people do, and

they have the credit-card bills to prove it. We live in a society where wealth is worshipped. So even if we can't afford the newest gadget or the current clothing fad, we'll go into debt to get it. The average American household owes more than $8,000 to credit-card companies. That's a lot of money!

After trying to live the lifestyle of the rich and famous, many people discover that things and money don't make them happy. Joy comes from the Lord. Happiness flows from being closely connected to family, friends, and other people in your life.

Thousands of middle schoolers and high schoolers go on missions trips every year. On these trips they come face-to-face with extreme poverty and are often surprised by the joy of the people they're serving. These people often don't know where their next meal is coming from and live in tiny shacks. Yet joy springs from their faces because they know the Lord. The truth is if you have God, that's all you need. Hebrews 13:5 (ESV) says, "Keep your life free from love of money, and be content with what you have, for [God] has said, 'I will never leave you nor forsake you.' "

Notice the words "be content." We're often discontent because we're jealous of our friends' smartphones or athletic shoes. Or maybe we get caught up wanting what we see in commercials. The Bible warns us of the dangers of jealousy. It's a green monster that robs us of joy and makes us want more.

When we're envious of someone else's life or possessions, it's as if we're discounting God's blessings in our lives. It's almost as if we're saying, "I need more. God, You're not giving me enough."

Instead of sending that message to our heavenly Father, our

words and actions should communicate two simple yet powerful words: "Thank You."

That's being content. And that's the greatest feeling.

God's Guide

Read: 1 Timothy 6:6–9

1. According to these verses, what things do you need in life to be content? Do you agree with that?

   _____

   _____

   _____

2. How can wanting to be rich lead to a trap? What are some better things you can pursue?

   _____

   _____

   _____

BONUS ACTIVITY

See how many coins you can balance on your elbow and then catch in your hand. The record is 212 by Great Britain's Dean Gould. To see an instructional video on the science behind this trick, search online for "How to catch coins falling from your elbow" and watch a minute-and-a-half video on Videojug.

Vexed by a Text

i got my first text message last week! Excitedly I opened it and read, "Where'd U get ur big teeth? At a fence board company?"

At first I thought, *I didn't know Grandpa has my cell number!*

He's always joking about my big teeth, and I'm always joking about his wrinkles.

Me: I think you stayed in the bath too long, Grandpa! You're all wrinkly!

Grandpa: I didn't take a bath. It's not the end of the month yet. But when I do, I'll need one of your baby teeth that fell out to float around on!

It's all harmless and fun—and sometimes stinky. But I realized it couldn't be Grandpa texting me. He's not really into technology. He just learned how to use the microwave. Plus, I don't think his phone can text. He's got a strange cell phone called a "land line" that's attached to the wall in his house.

Anyway, back to my first text. I'd sent several texts when I first got my phone.

"Hey, Wendy. Txt me!"

Instead of texting, she just leaned over and wrote on my arm. "There. You've been texted."

I guess she doesn't like receiving texts at lunch, especially when she's sitting across the table from me.

The next evening I texted her: "In the movies so I can't text. Talk to U L8R."

No reply. Later she told me she didn't text back because she knew I couldn't answer. That night I texted her, "Not at a movie, so I can txt now!"

She didn't reply then either. Later I found out she was at the movies. My text messaging wasn't off to a great start . . . until this text about my teeth came in. But it didn't bring the joy I was hoping for.

Sure, my teeth are kind of big. But now someone was making fun of them. I didn't know what to do, so I texted back, "I like my teeth."

I instantly got a reply: "Astronauts like them 2. Cause they can C them from space."

"Who is this?" I replied.

"Not ur dentist. He's icing down his fingers from the last time he worked on ur horse teeth."

"Keep it up," I texted back, "and I'll smile at u when the sun's out and blind u 4 life!"

That's when I heard Donny laugh from across the room. And I saw him look at his phone.

I'd heard about cyberbullying before, but I thought my teachers were talking about mean robots. Turns out cyberbullying is a huge

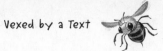

problem in our country. And not just Texas. Other countries as well! Mean kids send hurtful messages through text, Facebook, and Twitter. And I'd just become the next victim.

"What's the big deal, Donny?" I whispered across the room.

"I don't know what you're talking about," he whispered back.

I quickly texted the number again, and his phone vibrated.

"I knew it was you!" I shouted.

You know how there are times to stand up for yourself and times to let stuff go? Well, turns out this was a time to let things go . . . at least until everyone finished their tests.

"Bob," my teacher said, "you're supposed to be taking a test, and you're not supposed to have your phone out!"

After class I went to apologize to my teacher. As I explained about the texts, she shouted again.

"DONNY!"

Donny tried to deny it. He had a good argument. We all knew he didn't know how to spell *astronaut*. Then I remembered about AutoCorrect. AutoCorrect is a feature on your phone that tries to correct your misspelled words. But it doesn't always work.

Yesterday I sent a text to Wendy that was supposed to say, *"Don't forget 2 do ur art assignment 4 tomorrow!"* But AutoCorrect changed it to, *"I really like U! Can I go 2 the movies with U next time?"*

That technology still has some bugs to be worked out.

But Donny finally admitted what he did.

Turns out the school doesn't put up with bullying of any kind. They called a meeting with me, Donny, and both of our parents.

Donny quickly apologized to me. He said he didn't think about how mean it really was or how it made others feel.

And here's the best part! My school decided to hold an anti-bullying assembly. We got out of school for two hours! Everyone in school thought I was a hero.

Afterward I walked up to Donny, gave him a big smile, and said, "No hard feelings?"

"Yeah, no hard feelings," he said, shielding his eyes from the glare.

Super Average Advice

A late-night talk-show host once joked that YouTube, Twitter, and Facebook had agreed to merge into one super, time-wasting website.

The name? "YouTwitFace."

While that may be funny, you're seriously being a "TwitFace" if you're involved in bullying of any kind.

When your parents were growing up, bullying was limited to face-to-face conflicts. Sometimes the abuse was verbal. Other times things got physical. Today bullying can come from miles away as messages fly over phones or through the Internet. But cyberbullying can hurt just as much as physical bullying—maybe even more, because it can feel like you're being ganged up on.

One survey on cyberbullying found that eight out of 10 kids said their friends cyberbullied other kids because they thought it was funny. But hurting somebody is never funny. In fact, God wants you to act in the exact opposite way. First Thessalonians 5:11 says, "Encourage one another and build each other up as you are already doing."

Bullying doesn't build up. It tears down. And cyberbullying is a huge problem. In the cyberbullying survey, more than 40 percent of teens said they had been victims of cyberbullying in the past year. The other 60 percent were probably too busy texting to answer.

So what can you do to stop cyberbullying?

1. Think about whether your text or post could hurt someone before you send it. You never know what will be forwarded and shared with a person you didn't want to see it.

2. Talk to your parents. Only 25 percent of kids said they would tell an adult if they're being cyberbullied. Your parents can help. Let them know what you're dealing with.

Did You Know?

- The average teenager sends 60 texts a day. That's nearly 2,000 a month!
- In 2012, Austin Wierschke of Rhinelander, Wisconsin, was declared the fastest texter in America. He's won the LG US National Texting Championship twice! He practices by sending 500 texts a day.
- Experts estimate that six billion text messages are sent in the United States every day. If those texts were put in a straight line . . . it'd be a very long line.

3. Keep your password secret and your phone away from friends. Some kids like to sneak onto their friends' accounts and send mean or embarrassing messages. Those things can't be taken back and are often hurtful.

The Internet and smartphones are amazing tools for communication and knowledge. Be responsible as you use them. And remember that you represent Christ in everything you do—even when you're sending text messages.

God's Guide

Read: Proverbs 6:16–19

1. How do you think these verses relate to bullying? Write down some of the ways:

    _____

    _____

    _____

2. Bullies put down other people and make them feel bad. If you've ever bullied someone, put together a plan to apologize and make that person feel better.

    _____

    _____

    _____

BONUS ACTIVITY

Try to think of a worse job than making smartphone apps for babies.

Tech Takeover

"Are you boys still playing that video game?" Billy's dad, Mr. Lime, said when he walked into the family room.

"Yes, sir," Billy replied. "I just got it and want to see how far I can get."

"You got it two days ago!" Mr. Lime said.

"What day is it?" I asked.

"Saturday," he answered absurdly.

Turns out it wasn't so absurd. It was Saturday. Any video game that allows kids to time-travel should come with a warning label!

Two weeks ago I spent a few nights with Billy while my parents went on a "kid-free" trip. I thought my brother and I would be traveling for free with them. My parents and the cruise ship had a different idea entirely. Who knew anniversaries were so important?

Anyway, I was excited to stay with Billy and play his new video game, Dirt Bike Derby. In it you race a dirt bike through different levels. The best part is when you crash, it just starts over. It's not like real life. You don't have to fix your bike, apologize to the people whose property you're on, and ask them to take you to the hospital. This game saved countless injuries. But it also cost a lot of hours. I couldn't believe it was Saturday.

"Go outside," Mr. Lime said. "Get some exercise."

"You know how many calories I'm burning riding this bike up a mountain?" Billy said, working his video controller.

"Well, at least talk to each other," Mr. Lime said. "It's too quiet. Last time you two were quiet like this, I had to rebuild my fence."

"Sorry about that, Mr. Lime," I said. "That bicycle slingshot was a bad idea. But we did put the fence back up before you got home."

"I remember," he replied. "That's why I had to rebuild it. Not only were several of the boards broken, but I also had to buy a new stapler. Fences need nails, you know."

Billy and I knew he was right. We needed to do something else. Twenty minutes later, Mr. Lime came in to check on us. "I thought you were going outside. What are you doing?"

"Texting," Billy replied.

"Texting who?"

"Average Boy."

"He's right there!" Mr. Lime said, pointing at me.

(I'd like to point out that I think that's how the conversation went. I was busy texting Billy, so I'm not sure I heard everything correctly.)

Billy and I finally got up and walked outside. The graphics were amazing. The sun was bright. The breeze was gentle and light.

"What do you want to do?" I asked.

"Want to go see if Glasses McQueen has any new video games?" Billy said as his thumbs twitched.

"What's wrong with your thumbs?" I asked.

"I guess they're just used to having a controller in them."

That's when I remembered something my dad said the previous week.

"When Jesus comes back, I bet some kids are going to miss the awesomeness of it," he joked. "They'll be too busy tweeting and texting 'Jesus is back! Here's an Instagram photo of Jesus. Let's get Jesus trending on Twitter!'"

We should live our lives, not report about them. I don't want to miss out on any adventures because I'm sitting in front of some tiny screen.

With that in mind, I asked Billy, "Do you think technology is taking over our lives?"

"No way," he said. "That's a myth grown-ups made up years ago."

"Where'd you hear that?"

"I read it on Twitter."

That was it. I realized we couldn't have a conversation without involving technology. Billy and I decided right then to go a week without looking at any screens. Well, guess what? It was awesome!

We went to Mrs. Fox's house. She told us about the time she got locked inside the chicken coop when she was little.

"I had to eat raw eggs just to stay alive!" she said.

"How long were you in there?" I asked.

"About twenty minutes," she said with a laugh.

Mr. Lime taught us how to change the oil in his car. Mrs. Lime showed me how to get oil out of my shirt. Billy and I fished and hiked. It was the best seven days ever, because we were living life instead of playing it. If life was a video game, we both got high scores that week!

Super Average Advice

Some kids can be addicted to technology without even knowing it. See if you relate to any of these statements:

- If you think about playing video hockey as you play the real sport, you may be a tech addict.
- If you wish you could be more like your online video-game character, you may be a tech addict.

Did You Know?

- On average, eight- to 12-year-olds play video games 13 hours a week.*
- Doctors are diagnosing more and more kids with "Nintendo thumb"—a repetitive strain injury caused by too much time with a controller in their hands. *Wiiitis* is also on the increase, causing sore shoulders and elbows from waving around a Wii game controller.
- The American Academy of Pediatrics says children should spend less than two hours a day using technology. That includes video games, TV, computers, and videos.

* Unless they get a new video game; then they play 13 hours a day!

- If you watch a squirrel and start looking around for a way to pause it, you may be a tech addict.
- If school seems meaningless because it takes a whole year to go up a level, you may be a tech addict.
- If your neck hurts from always looking down at your phone or PSP (PlayStation Portable), you may be a tech addict.
- If your fish dies and you stare at it waiting for it to spring back to life, you may be a tech addict.
- If you're more concerned about your online friends than your real-life ones, you may be a tech addict.

You've grown up in a world of technology. Smartphones, laptop computers, the Internet, Facebook. Technology isn't bad. It's actually pretty amazing. It puts information at our fingertips, speeds up communication, and often comes with awesome graphics. Doctors can even operate by remote control from hundreds of miles away using robot hands to save lives. Fortunately, students can't do that—otherwise they'd never get out of bed!

But technology can be dangerous when it takes over your life.

In 1 Corinthians 6:12, the apostle Paul wrote, " 'Everything is permissible for me,' but not everything is helpful. 'Everything is permissible for me,' but I will not be brought under the control of anything." As a Christian, you don't have to follow all the Old Testament rules. But as Paul pointed out, just because something is okay to do doesn't mean it's helpful. And it's doubly important that nothing takes control of your life, like video games or technology.

So what can you do?

Set limits. Decide how much time is too much time to spend playing video games, watching TV, or updating your social-media page. A parent can help you decide what's best. Once you reach your limit, find something else to do. Read a book, ride a bike, bake some cookies, or hang out with friends. And that leads to the second point . . .

Make friends. Not online friends. Real flesh-and-blood friends are the best. If you talk all the time online or through texting, you may actually end up feeling more lonely than if you spend face time with friends. Find friends who share your interests, encourage you to grow closer to God, and can help you escape the trap of technology.

God's Guide

Read: 2 Timothy 2:22

1. What are some "youthful passions" that the apostle Timothy is asking you to "flee from"? Would video games count?

   _____

   _____

   _____

2. What's the best way to "pursue righteousness, faith, love, and peace"? Does God want you to do this alone or with a friend?

   _____

   _____

   _____

BONUS ACTIVITY

Go outside and do three things you've never done before. Then go to *averageboy.org*, click on "Ask Average Boy," and tell me what you did! If it's really strange, Billy and I may do it, and I'll write about it in a future issue of *Adventures in Odyssey Clubhouse* magazine!

Just Take a Mulligan

ou're supposed to yell four!" my brother shouted at me.

"Don't you mean *fore*?" I said, correcting my brother's verbal spelling.

"That's what I said!" he screamed, even more upset than before.

"Wutever," I said, spelling it wrong in my head just for fun.

My brother and I rarely fight. In fact, we never fight unless we're actually near each other. And at that moment, he was sitting on my chest.

You see, I accidentally hit him with a golf ball at this really professional and difficult golf course. My accuracy surprised even me. I'd never hit a ball that far or that straight before. Even the owner of Putt-Putt Golf Park was impressed.

I'd been trying to hit my ball into a mechanical alligator's mouth. Well, this alligator must've been on a hunger strike, because it kept closing its mouth every time my ball got anywhere near it. Billy suggested I walk up and place the ball in its mouth. But thanks to a nature show I'd just watched about an alligator wrestler named Big Jim No Fingers, I knew that was a bad idea.

Instead I hauled back and swung as hard as I could. The ball flew into the air and right toward my brother, who was standing two holes away eating a snow cone. I knew I was supposed to yell something, so I yelled, "Hey!"

If you're ever in this situation, don't yell, "Hey!" It just makes the person turn toward you.

Smack! The ball hit my brother square in the chest, and he took off running toward me.

"Look, he's bringing my golf ball back," I said to Billy. "What a nice brother."

"Uh, he didn't pick up your ball," Billy said, "and he looks pretty mad."

My brother dove at me, knocking both of us to the ground. As we fell, his ball flew out of his hand and into the alligator's mouth. Now I was mad! The gator finally got hungry in the middle of my fight.

I was also mad because my brother smashed his snow cone into my forehead. I'd never had brain freeze on the outside of my head before, and I didn't like it. Losing my temper, I flung my brother off me.

"I'm taking a mulligan," I said.

My brother didn't know what a mulligan was, so he thought I had called him a name.

"You're a mulligan head!" he shouted.

I started to correct him, but then I noticed that everyone at the putt-putt course had stopped to watch us. I quickly got embarrassed.

Brothers shouldn't act this way, especially Christian brothers.

I turned to the gathering crowd and said, "Thank you! Thank you! This concludes our new play, *The Ball That Came from Nowhere.* We hope you enjoyed it."

My brother also realized we were making a scene, so he whispered, "But the ball didn't come from nowhere. It came from you!"

"Yeah, I'm so sorry. I wasn't trying to hit you. You know I'm not good enough to hit you with a ball on purpose. Believe me, I've tried . . . uh, I mean I'm not good at golf. I'll even buy you a new snow cone."

I could see him calming down.

"What's a mulligan anyway?" he asked.

"It's a do-over," I explained. "In golf you can call a mulligan, and what just happened doesn't count."

"Can I get a mulligan on tackling you?" he asked as we walked over to the snow-cone stand. "I sort of slowed down on my approach."

That made me laugh.

Did You Know?

- In the late 1800s, the sport of miniature golf was invented when short golf holes were created on grass putting greens. Rails, mechanical alligators, and windmills were added many years later.
- Women first played miniature golf—not regular golf—because it was considered unladylike to lift the club past their shoulders.
- Tackling someone is not a proper response to being angry . . . unless you're playing football.

My brother and I have been fighting a lot less lately because we realized that nothing good happens when we're mad.

I think Satan loves it when we lose our cool. Anger can be a seed that grows into a tangled mess, choking out the joy from our lives. So when you start getting mad, stop and take a mulligan. Just start over and act more like Christ.

I was in the middle of buying my brother another snow cone when Billy suddenly hollered, "Hey!" I turned just in time to see his ball hit me in the leg.

"I mean fore!" Billy said.

I guess I wasn't the only one tormented by that alligator!

Super Average Advice

In Jesus' famous Sermon on the Mount, He passed down some serious godly wisdom. Jesus was like, *Bang!* And the people were like, *What?!?* when He said these words:

- The gentle are blessed, for they will inherit the earth (Matthew 5:5).
- The merciful are blessed, for they will be shown mercy (Matthew 5:7).
- The peacemakers are blessed, for they will be called sons of God (Matthew 5:9).

Nowhere did Jesus say, "If somebody's a jerk, be a jerk back." Instead, God's Son said, "If anyone slaps you on your right cheek, turn the other to him also" (Matthew 5:39).

When somebody says something mean to you or hurts you, it's

natural to want to lash out. But before you do, think about Jesus' high standard for your behavior. Then use these two tips to handle conflict in your own life.

Be slow to anger. You'll have a hard time following Jesus' command to be gentle and merciful if you rely only on your own strength. Only the Holy Spirit can help you show love to those who hurt you. Getting angry doesn't benefit anybody. James 1:19–20 tells us, "Everyone must be quick to hear, slow to speak, and slow to anger, for man's anger does not accomplish God's righteousness."

By controlling your emotions and being slow to anger, you'll be able to speak rationally instead of acting irrationally—just like Lexie does here:

Julie: You're a booger head!

Lexie: I'm sad that you have to be mean to make yourself feel good, Julie. But I'm not going to be a jerk. I'm going to show you respect.

Julie: Wha—?

When you listen first, speak clearly, and don't get angry, you'll defuse conflicts before they start. Plus, a lot of times people act mean just to get a reaction out of you. Don't let them win by giving them the negative reaction they want.

Be a peacemaker. Which sounds better, being a peacemaker or a fool? The answer is obvious: Peacemakers are blessed, while fools suffer harm. Proverbs 20:3 tells us, "It is honorable for a man to resolve a dispute, but any fool can get himself into a quarrel."

Fighting and getting physical is easy. Showing self-control can be hard. But you'll create stronger relationships in life when you're able to talk through your problems and find solutions without getting mad.

God's Guide

Read: Romans 12:17–18

1. According to these verses, what should you do if someone is mean to you?

   _____

   _____

   _____

2. What are some ways to live at peace with everyone? Does this mean you should run away from problems or talk them over with people face-to-face?

   _____

   _____

   _____

BONUS ACTIVITY

Tie golf clubs to your and a friend's legs. Have a Frankenstein walking race to see who can get around your house first. Be careful not to hurt yourself or the clubs . . . especially if they're your dad's.

A Narrow Path to Victory

I wanted to write about my experience at science camp. But my mom said everyone had already read about it in the newspaper. I should've been more careful. Those Bunsen burners sure live up to their name.

Anyway, I'm really enjoying getting into nature, so I thought I'd write about that instead. My dad and I entered a bike race! Actually, I entered us to surprise my dad. He was so surprised that his face turned red with excitement.

"What? Four miles!" he screamed. "*Ugh!* Why?"

We have a tandem bike, which is a regular bike with a smaller bike attached behind it. My dad sits in front and pedals. I sit in back to help balance. If you don't have a bike like this, you should get one. My dad said you can have ours, but I know he's joking. He's been really funny since the doctor gave him those pain pills, but that's getting ahead of the story.

The people organizing the race provided a list of rules and items

to bring. Since this was a gift for my dad, I bought everything on the list using the money I made mowing lawns.

The first thing was water. Did you know a gallon of water costs 65 cents, but a small bottle of water costs $1.08? That's crazy! My dad didn't raise a money waster, so I bought the gallon jug and two straws.

The list also said to bring helmets. Looking back, I should have brought my dad's bicycle helmet. His motorcycle helmet weighed eight pounds more, but Dad looked way cooler than the other riders. Plus, his neck is really muscular right now!

When we arrived at the race, we saw eight other father-son teams. Instantly I felt we'd win. They all had small bottles of water. *Ha!* Obviously they weren't very smart and didn't know the value of a dollar!

We all lined up, and a man shot a small gun to start the race.

"Hey, Dad!" I began to say.

"No," he shouted, "you can't have a gun like that."

My dad knows me really well.

About 10 minutes into the race, my dad started getting into the competition.

"Drink water," he panted. "We're too heavy!"

I pulled out our jug and started guzzling water. Three minutes later, I had to go to the bathroom. After a quick stop, we were back in the race . . . sort of. We were *waaay* behind the other teams.

My dad was getting frustrated, but I had a plan. I knew a short-cut! I waited until the right moment and then shouted, "Lean right!" Then I used the weight of our water jug to help us make a tight turn.

Suddenly we went speeding through the woods on a secret path only I knew about. The tree limbs had grown since I'd last been on that path, which is why I was glad to be wearing a bike helmet.

Tree limbs, insects, and one shocked squirrel clawed at our faces. I bet my dad was glad he had on his motorcycle helmet now!

Did You Know?

- To stay properly hydrated, doctors recommend that you drink at least two eight-ounce cups of water a couple of hours before you exercise. Drink an additional cup 15 minutes before you start. Then drink eight more ounces of water for every 15 minutes you exercise.
- The LoToJa Classic is the longest one-day, amateur bicycle race sanctioned by USA Cycling. Going from Logan, Utah, to Jackson Hole, Wyoming, the race covers 206 miles.
- The first tandem bicycles were introduced in the 1890s.

Anyway, we jolted out of the forest onto the main road in front of everyone! In fact, we almost hit Donny, the school bully, and his dad.

"Here, Donny," I said, handing him my water jug.

Donny looked confused but then grabbed it.

This lightened our load and made my dad's pedaling work even better. Moments later we crossed the finish line in first place! I was so excited that I jumped off our bike, forgetting that it was my job to balance.

The bike instantly fell over. Fortunately it didn't end up with a scratch on it, because my dad cushioned it from hitting the road.

"Are you okay, Dad?" I shouted.

"We won!" he yelled back. "Now help me lift my head so I can get my helmet off."

You see, before the race I had carefully read the rules, which said that tiny paths through the woods were legal.

This reminded me of the Bible verse: "For the gate is wide and the road is broad that leads to destruction, and there are many who go through it. How narrow is the gate and difficult the road that leads to life, and few find it" (Matthew 7:13–14).

I found the road that leads to victory. Twice! Anyway, I have to go find Donny. I'm really thirsty.

Super Average Advice

Have you ever hiked through a forest? When you find a wide path, you know a lot of people have gone that way before you. A well-worn trail is usually the easiest way to go.

But God doesn't call us to an easy life. He calls us to a life filled with adventure!

A narrow path is harder to fit through. You have to give more effort to walk a difficult road. In the end, however, you'll avoid destruction and reap great rewards for following the Lord (see Matthew 7:13–14).

Do you ever wish you could ask Jesus why living for Him is harder than just going along with the crowd? One reason may be that things of value are worth working for. Maybe this scene from Luke 9:57–58 will give you more insight:

Unnamed person: "I will follow You wherever You go!"

Jesus: "Thanks, can you carry My backpack?"

Actually, that's *not* what Jesus said. Instead of being excited that someone wanted to enthusiastically follow Him, He said, "Foxes have dens, and birds of the sky have nests, but the Son of Man has no place to lay His head."

In other words, God's Son was saying, "Don't get so gung ho, Junior. It's going to be a bumpy road. You sure you know what you're signing up for?"

If your life feels kind of bumpy every once in a while, don't worry. That's a good thing. You build strength by conquering adversity. Don't doubt God when the road gets rough. Just cling closer to Him.

Following Jesus means taking the narrow path. You'll have to make sacrifices for your faith. That may mean missing parties, going to church instead of hanging out with friends, or waking up extra early so you can start your day by reading the Bible and praying. Then there's the rejection or ridicule you might feel from other students—or even teachers—for your beliefs.

At the end of the journey, a difficult path brings benefits those on the easy road can't understand. Your joy will be deeper. Your adventures more fulfilling. Your life more meaningful.

So stay on the narrow path. It's the right way to go!

God's Guide

Read: Micah 6:8

1. What three things does the Lord want you to do?

   _____

   _____

   _____

2. Do you ever feel like you're alone on the narrow path? Read Hebrews 13:5. Write a prayer thanking God for always being with you as you follow Him.

   _____

   _____

   _____

BONUS ACTIVITY

Go on a bike ride with your family. Ride somewhere you've never been before and then see if you can find a short-cut home. (Just make sure you have a phone with you for when . . . er, *if* you get lost.)

Does School Bug You?

Let me see your bug-collection assignment," my dad said.

Happily I handed him the assignment.

"This is just the paper explaining how to do the assignment," he said. "I want to see your bugs."

"I'm starting later today," I said. "It's not due till the twenty-eighth."

"Today's the twenty-seventh!" Dad said.

People say the older you get, the faster time flies. That is so true! I thought I had weeks to work on my bug project. I told my dad not to panic as I ran to my room. Twenty minutes later, I came back with seven different bugs.

"Glad to see you're working on it," Dad said. "I'm proud of you."

The compliment was so nice that I didn't tell him I'd just found all the bugs in my room. But I did learn a valuable lesson. (Well, two lessons if you count the one about not leaving a sandwich near an open window.) The lesson was: I needed to better manage my homework.

Dad and I went outside and caught the rest of the bugs. I even caught a flea . . . twice! The first time, I saw a piece of black rice moving around on my dog. I knew from eating Chinese food that rice shouldn't move—or be black. I grabbed it with a pair of chopsticks and realized it was a flea. As I showed it to Dad, the flea escaped. Dad sure picked the wrong time to have a beard. I eventually caught it a second time, thanks to my dad giving me hints by scratching.

"I'm going to take these homework assignments more seriously," I told him.

"I'm going to go shave," Dad said.

We both went inside, and I started to work on a book report.

The book my teacher assigned was really long and boring. She said we could use outside resources for our book report, so I planned to watch the movie. But when I searched for a movie about the book, I discovered that one didn't exist. I assumed it was because the director kept falling asleep while reading the screenplay.

So for the rest of the night, I read. If I was going to get better at managing my homework, I had to start somewhere. The next day I read on the bus. I even read at recess and during lunch. The lunch part wasn't a great sacrifice. They were serving "Spaghetti Surprise," and I'd decided to eat gluten-free after I saw what it looked like.

My tray looked like 30 angry spiders wrestling in glue. Fortunately, I'd put the sandwich from my window in my backpack, so I munched on it while reading.

Surprisingly the book got interesting halfway through. Someone had drawn some stick-figure cartoons along the margin. The rest of the book, however, was terrible.

(Note: If you don't like this book, please draw some stick-figure cartoons in the margins so the next reader will enjoy it more.)

I finished the book on the bus ride home and wrote my report that night. I have to admit it felt good. I was taking my job of doing well in school seriously. The next day I bounded into English class and plopped my report on my teacher's desk.

"Wow, Bob!" She smiled. "I didn't expect to get your book report on time, much less early."

"That's right," I said. "I guess it *is* early, because the bell hasn't rung yet."

"Technically, that's true," my teacher said. "But I meant the report isn't due for another two weeks."

Did You Know?

- A survey at more than 770 universities found that one in five college students goes to class without completing his or her homework.
- More than 900,000 different types or species of insects live on earth, making them the most diverse living things on the planet.
- If you put a peanut butter and jelly sandwich in your backyard, you can discover more than 20 types of insects.*

*But you'll ruin a delicious sandwich.

That was it. I realized I needed help. I talked to Kelly, Karen, and Kim—the smartest girls in my class. They agreed to teach me how to manage my homework if I'd point out in this book that they are the smartest people in my class . . . boys and girls included.

They each used a daily planning calendar. Every day they took it out at the beginning of class. Then they wrote down all the assignments and when they were due. They set daily goals to finish assignments little by little.

I've been following their plan for a week now, and it's amazing!

Anyway, I need to go help Dad. He's trying to find the smell in the back of his car. I hope it's not an animal, because I left my bug project back there. I don't want anything messing with that!

Super Average Advice

Since the beginning of time, kids have gone to school. Acts 7:22 tells us that "Moses was educated in all the wisdom of the Egyptians." Can you imagine what homework was like for him?

Teacher: Tonight's homework assignment is to collect bugs.

Moses (thinking): *Hmm, if only I could find a swarm of gnats, flies, and locusts.*

Think how much easier that assignment would've been during the 10 plagues of Egypt. Just walk outside, and there's a swarm!

Love it or hate it, the fact is homework helps you learn. So instead of avoiding homework or putting it off until the last minute, try these four ways to score big on assignments:

1. *Pay attention and take notes in class.* The better you understand the assignment and what your teacher is looking for, the better you'll do.

2. *Organize your papers, assignments, and notes in folders and keep track of them in a planning calendar.* Then you'll easily be able to find what you're looking for when you get home, without adding any stress. Keeping things in order reflects God's character. As 1 Corinthians 14:33 says, "God is not a God of disorder but of peace."

3. *Manage your time.* Work on big projects a little bit at a time. Start early on reports and projects so they don't seem so overwhelming. Know when to say no to TV or hanging out with your friends. Then you can say yes to better grades.

4. *Make it fun.* Homework doesn't have to be horrible. Take breaks between assignments to listen to a song or talk with friends. Ask for tips from your parents. They'd probably love to help you and are interested in what you're learning. Add your personality to assignments when you can. If you like making movies, ask your teacher if you can create a film instead of doing a book report. If you're funny, add humor to your English assignments.

Doing well at homework isn't rocket science. (Although if you do really well at your homework, you could become a rocket scientist.) All it takes is persistence, perseverance, and organization.

God's Guide

Read: Luke 14:28–30

1. How is building a tower like completing a homework assignment? Why is it good to have a plan?

   _____

   _____

   _____

2. Why is it important to finish what you start? If you don't complete a project, what does that say about you?

   _____

   _____

   _____

BONUS ACTIVITY

Grab some cooked pasta and create your own "angry spider." Be creative!

The Smell of Success!

"What's that smell?" my mom asked.

"I don't smell anything," I said, sniffing the air.

"Well, that usually means it's you," Mom said, opening the windows. "What have you been doing?"

I took her through my day. Billy and I rode bikes to the city trash dump. We looked for a bike handle to replace my broken one. We also found half a can of paint that we used to paint most of our clubhouse. Then I helped Mrs. Fox give her dog a bath. Kyler called and invited me to see the pig he got to show for 4-H. We played pig rodeo for a bit. Wendy saw us as she rode by on her bike and stopped to cheer me on. At least, that's what I think she was doing. I couldn't really hear what she was saying because of all the mud in my ears. After that, my brother and I hiked through the moss beds at the creek to catch frogs.

So far I didn't see anything that would make me smell bad.

Mom disagreed. I didn't even get to tell her about the raccoon we found on the side of the road.

"Go take a bath!" she demanded.

That's happening a lot lately. The bath thing. Not finding the raccoon.

My parents warned me that my body would be going through all kinds of changes. Some have happened. Some haven't. For instance, my voice hasn't really gotten deeper. I thought I'd get a deep, manly voice. But people still mistake me on the phone for my Mom . . . or my baby sister. I don't even have a baby sister!

Billy's voice has gotten deeper. Almost too deep. His voice carries all over the town. Once he told me to get out of a tree. Before I could start climbing down, I saw kids all over the neighborhood climbing out of trees looking for their dads.

His voice actually changed in a matter of seconds.

"Why don't we make a ROPE SWING," he said.

"What's with your voice?" I asked.

"I DON'T KNOW. HEY, IT SOUNDS REALLY DEEP. WHY ARE YOU LOOKING AT ME LIKE THAT?"

"I just never thought I'd be friends with Darth Vader," I joked.

My parents did warn me that my body would start to stink. This worried me.

I didn't know if it would gradually get worse or happen all at once like Billy's voice.

My dad said not to worry. My mom bought me some spray deodorant. The directions said to hold the can about six inches from your armpit and press the button. Then, and this part isn't in the directions, you drop the can and run around the bathroom screaming because your armpit feels like it's being stung by icy bees!

From that moment on, I used roll-on deodorant.

The problem was I kept forgetting to put it on. My dad said to put it by my toothbrush so I wouldn't forget. We all had a good laugh at that.

But he was on to something. I needed to put it beside something I see every day, so I tied it around my dog's collar.

Did You Know?

- According to scientists, these are the stinkiest creatures on earth: (1) stink badger, (2) stinkbird, (3) stinkbug, (4) skunk, and (5) 11-year-old boy after hockey practice.*
- Mum deodorant was invented in 1888, becoming the first-ever commercially sold product to prevent body odor.
- Stoppette stopped people from smelling bad in the 1940s. That's when this first-of-its-kind spray deodorant hit stores.

*Okay, these aren't all scientific facts, but they're probably accurate.

My mom had a better idea. She put it on the table next to my breakfast. One morning I was so tired that I pulled off the cap and rubbed deodorant all over my pancakes.

Growing up can be a hard adjustment. You don't want to stink, but you don't to smell too good either. I found that out when Billy and I discovered an unopened bottle of cologne in the city trash dump. I couldn't believe someone would throw it away! I knew this cologne was expensive because I'd bought some just like it for my dad at the gas station.

The next week as I got ready for church, I sprayed the cologne all over my body. Suddenly I heard a scratching noise at the bathroom door. I told my brother I'd be out in a second, but the scratching continued. I opened the door and my dog tackled me. He kept sniffing and trying to roll on me.

"What's all the barking?" my dad asked, walking in. "Ugh! What'd the dog get into?"

"I think it's my cologne," I said, showing him the bottle.

"Where'd you get that?" he said. "I thought I threw that . . . uh, away after I used it all."

After my second shower, we headed to church. Dad even let me ride in the very back of the truck. My hair looked great, and I didn't even comb it.

Super Average Advice

When it comes to smelling good and feeling clean, this poem may help:

Jonathan Miller Michael McGrath
Simply refused to take a bath.
He liked to do what other boys did,
And overall was a pretty good kid.
His hair was combed and face free of zits
But a horrible odor came from his pits.
His grandma said, "You smell like a dog,"
When she came to visit and entered his fog.
He said in reply, "Just let me be!
Soap and water are the great enemy."
Then something strange happened one day,
When he took his shirt off—it walked away.
He'd never seen his clothes act so weird.
He scratched his chin and removed a "dirt beard."
Finally, Jonathan said with a laugh,
"Okay, now it's time. I'll take a bath."

Hopefully, you're not like Jonathan but bathe before your
clothes develop minds of their own. Taking care of your physical
body is important. Your appearance matters because it'll draw people
to you or cause them to turn away . . . and in some cases, run away!

God wants us to be good stewards of everything He gives us.
That includes our money, our possessions, and our bodies. You
wouldn't leave a brand-new bike out in the rain to rust or flush $20
down the toilet. In the same way, you need to take care of your body
by eating right, sleeping enough, and keeping it clean and sparkly.
(Okay, maybe not sparkly . . . except your teeth.)

You honor God by taking care of your body. He created you perfectly. As your body changes, it'll take some getting used to. Growing and developing are just part of becoming the person God is making you to be. You're a work in progress, and that's okay.

So don't get discouraged as you go through this time in your life. Just keep working on yourself and growing closer to God—and don't forget that deodorant is your friend!

God's Guide

Read: 1 Corinthians 6:20

1. What does this verse mean when it says, "You were bought at a price"?

   _____

   _____

   _____

   _____

   _____

2. What are some ways you can glorify God with your body? List at least five different ways.

   _____

   _____

   _____

   _____

   _____

·······BONUS QUESTION·······

Do you really think people rubbed roses under their arms
to smell good before someone invented deodorant? Try it.
Just make sure not to use poison ivy. Trust me!

Committed!

I think I need to be more reliable. I came to this conclusion because of something my dad said.

"You need to be more reliable," he said after I forgot to feed the dog again.

He was in the middle of telling me how I'd been slacking off on my chores lately. I started to point out a few things I hadn't forgotten. But when I started talking, Dad stopped me.

"I can tell you even forgot to brush your teeth today," he added.

I didn't bother to tell him that he didn't need to use the word *today*.

As always, Dad was right. So I made a list of all the things I needed to remember. It was a great list. I was really proud of it. Too bad I lost it before I could write down "Keep track of list" on it.

I was determined to be more reliable. So when Mrs. Dodd asked me to house-sit for her, I instantly said yes. This was my opportunity to show my reliability! Plus, I'd always wanted to get up on Mrs. Dodd's roof. When I asked where she kept her ladder, she informed me that *house-sitting* doesn't mean sitting on a house. I was supposed to sit *in* her house. My main job was to watch and feed her cats. I also needed to bring in several boxes that would be delivered while she was gone.

I'm going to be honest. I love helping out, but I'm not a big fan of cats. Cats run from me. I once tried to make friends with my cat by putting some tuna in his bowl. But he just darted from under the couch, ate the tuna, and then ran away from me . . . now with bad breath. I wonder how long it's been since he brushed his teeth.

But reliable people don't turn down difficult jobs, so I went to Mrs. Dodd's house in the morning. She showed me where everything was and said she'd be back late that night. I asked important questions to show her how serious I was about this job, such as "Which remote do I use to watch TV?"

Three hours later, I was getting really good at house-sitting. I'd been sitting the entire time! Every once in a while her cats would wander into the room to check on me and go *Scccccaaaahhhhhhh*, which I think means "Welcome to our house."

Suddenly the doorbell rang. The first package had arrived! I brought it inside. Being reliable felt good. Then my phone vibrated. I walked over and saw Wendy's picture on my phone screen. She had texted me! I couldn't believe it. I had been waiting for this. I called Billy to share the news.

"What'd it say?" he asked.

"Oh, I forgot to look at it," I said. "I'll call you back."

I opened my text and saw: "Hey, AB. Going with some friends 2 the park. Come hang out!"

This was awesome! I couldn't wait to show off the half chin-up I could do on the monkey bars, thanks to my ever-growing muscles—and the fact that they lowered the chin-up bar to where I can stand most of the way up!

Sccccaaaahhhhhhh.

I looked over at the cats and came back to reality. I was house-sitting. I couldn't go. I had cats to watch and had to bring in two more packages. I fell back on the couch, grabbed my phone, and texted, "Hey, Wendy. I'm watching Mrs. Dodd's cats all day, and she's got some boxes being delivered. I think she picked me because the boxes r super heavy. The first one is here and must weigh at least 4 pounds! Sorry, I can't make it."

I felt horrible until my phone vibrated again.

Wendy texted back: "I think she picked u because u r a man of ur word. Nice job putting ur commitments 1st!"

Did you hear that? Of course you didn't. This is a book. But did you read that?! She called me a *man*! The rest of the day went great. I watered Mrs. Dodd's plants without being asked and even cleaned

Did You Know?

- House sitters can earn $15 a day or more.
- Cats are more popular than dogs. Americans own more than 95 million cats as pets, compared to 83 million dogs.
- Climbing ladders resulted in almost 250,000 emergency-room visits in 2012—proving that literal house-sitting can be dangerous.

her kitchen. I knew she wouldn't notice, because she wasn't there when I spilled all that orange juice. But it still felt great!

When Mrs. Dodd got home, she looked at all her deliveries and said, "It's so nice having someone living close by that I can rely on. Thank you for getting my packages and feeding my cats."

Oh. Feed the cats, I thought. *No wonder they kept hissing at me!*

Super Average Advice

Jesus loved to tell stories with deep meanings. The Bible calls these parables. One of His parables featured a pair of brothers. Let's call them Rex and Reginald. (You can read about them in Matthew 21:28–31.)

"Hey, Rex," Dad said. "I need you to help me with some gardening today."

"First of all, thanks for not naming me Reginald. Second of all, I can't," Rex said. "All my buddies are playing ultimate Frisbee. We're going to play for two hours and then look up the word *ultimate* to make sure we're doing it right."

Dad didn't like Rex's answer, so he went to find Reginald. Reginald sat behind his neat desk reading a book (just for fun let's say it was *Devotions for Super Average Kids: Book One*).

"Reginald, can you help with some gardening today?" Dad asked.

"Of course, Father," Reginald said. "I live to serve. By the way, you should read this book. It's awesome!"

At the garden, Rex rolled up on his skateboard, deciding to skip Frisbee and help out his dad. Reginald was a no-show.

So who did the father's will? The son who showed no interest in working but then showed up, or the son who said he'd be there and wasn't? Whose actions are more disappointing to you?

Even though neither son kept his word, at least Rex came and helped out. And that's what the father wanted. Reginald, although he tried to play the perfect son, didn't follow through on his promise.

God wants us to be true to our word. When we keep our commitments, we help other people and ourselves—because it feels great to be reliable.

Being reliable means you're trustworthy. In the Greek, the word *trustworthy* means "worthy of being trusted" (or something like that). People don't automatically give you their trust. You earn their trust by keeping your commitments.

God always keeps His promises to us. He is 100 percent trustworthy. As we keep our promises to our parents, teachers, friends, and family, we reflect God's character and grow to be more like Him.

Of course, it's not always easy to do what you said you'd do. Different things can come up—even fun things. At those times, you'll have to make a decision to follow fun or follow through. Because following fun often isn't the choice that receives the most rewards.

Which would you rather do?

- Finish chores or hang out with friends?
- Walk the dog or play a video game?
- Read the Bible or eat ice cream?

Wait! you may be thinking. *What does reading the Bible have to do with making a promise?*

A lot. When you prayed to invite Jesus Christ into your life and follow Him, you committed your life to God. Part of that commitment meant learning more about Him. By going to church, reading the Bible, and praying, you're following through on your promise to God. And that's the most important promise of all! It's the ultimate! (Yes, that word's used correctly.)

God's Guide

Read: Numbers 30:1–2

1. These verses tell us to not break our word. Have you ever said one thing and then done another (or forgot to do what you said)? If so, what happened?

   _____

   _____

   _____

2. Why do you think God wants us to keep our promises to Him and to other people?

   _____

   _____

   _____

BONUS ACTIVITY

Next time you see a cat walking around outside, run up and go *Sccccaaaahhhhhhh!* to welcome it to the neighborhood.

13

Mannequins, Mall Cops, and Me... Oh My!

As I waited in a line at the mall to buy a shirt, people kept walking by and laughing. I didn't see what was so funny. Waiting in line is the worst, and this line wasn't moving! I continued to wait while texting on my phone. That's when my youth leader, Tim, showed up.

"What are you doing?" he asked.

"I'm waiting in line to buy this shirt."

"Uh, you're standing behind a row of mannequins," Tim said.

I looked up and saw nine mannequins all facing the same way, with me at the end. So that's why people were laughing! It also explained why the line wasn't moving.

How embarrassing! Tim said it wasn't a big deal. Before heading to the cash register, I decided to move the mannequins so other people wouldn't be confused. Tim didn't think that would be a problem, but I wanted to make sure.

I grabbed the one closest to me and started to twist it. This mannequin obviously worked out. It was way heavier than I expected. Before I could move it, it fell forward and . . . have you ever lined up dominoes in a long row and then knocked one down? Let me tell you, it's way cooler with mannequins.

Not everybody agreed. This lady shopper had just walked up to feel the shirt of the last mannequin. That's when my domino effect caused it to lurch at her. She must've thought it was coming to life, because she fainted and fell back into a display of shirts. Tim caught her before she hit the ground, so no one was hurt.

However, the mall security guard wasn't happy. He pointed out that he got hurt when he fell out of his chair.

You see, the scream from the lady woke up the security guy. His chair was leaning against the wall. When he jolted awake, he fell on the floor. Everyone in the store laughed. I even thought I heard one of the mannequins giggle a little bit.

I wasn't laughing. The security guard yelled at me and blamed me for wrecking the place. I guess he had a point, but it was an accident. I began to worry about going to mall prison. I envisioned myself in a mall prison uniform folding new clothes for stores. Or maybe I'd be forced to model clothes like one of the mannequins!

"Hi, I'm Tim." My youth leader stepped in just then. "I'm Bob's youth pastor, and I saw the whole thing. It was an accident. Bob shouldn't have touched the mannequin, but it was an honest mistake. We'll be glad to put everything back in place."

"Yeah," I jumped in, "I'll even tell you a bedtime story so you can get back to your nap."

My youth leader quickly put his hand over my mouth. He does that a lot.

Anyway, we restored the store, and I thanked my youth leader for helping out. He does that a lot too. Besides my parents, he's the best mentor I have. He gives me daily Bible verses to study, is always there when I need someone to talk to, and offers great advice to keep me out of trouble . . . well, sometimes.

The security guard decided I didn't have to go to mall prison as long as I fixed everything. Tim and I set the mannequins back up. Then Tim helped the lady who fainted carry her bags to her car.

Everything was going great until I walked out of the store and the security alarm went off. I really wished I'd remembered to pay for that shirt!

Super Average Advice

Have you ever tried to put together a gigantic puzzle? Figuring out where the pieces fit isn't easy. A picture of what it's supposed to look like helps. But what if you can't see the picture?

That's where mentors come in. They can see the big picture. Mentors are older and wiser people in our lives who can help encourage us. Our lives are like a puzzle that we put together day by day. Sometimes it can feel as if we don't know where the pieces fit, so it's great to have someone in our lives who knows what the finished puzzle should look like.

A mentor may be a parent, grandparent, youth leader, trusted neighbor, or family friend. The key is it should be somebody who knows you and knows God.

The Bible features tons of examples of good mentors. Moses mentored Joshua, who led God's people into the Promised Land. The prophet Elijah mentored Elisha, helping him become a voice for God among his people. Jesus mentored His disciples. They learned wisdom from God's Son through His words and actions.

Then there was the apostle Paul, who wrote a majority of the New Testament. When Paul popped up in the Bible, he was persecuting and imprisoning Christ's followers. But once Paul met the risen Lord on the road to Damascus, he gave his life to Jesus. After Christ changed Paul's heart, Barnabas acted as a mentor to Paul. Barnabas traveled to Jerusalem to speak on Paul's behalf and move him safely to Tarsus (Acts 9:27–30). Later, Barnabas came back to Tarsus to find Paul and take him to Antioch, where they preached together for an entire year (Acts 11:25–26).

Once Paul grew more mature in his faith, he played the role of

Did You Know?

- The role of a mentor is to teach and advise in an honest way, while maintaining confidentiality.
- As a mentee, or a person being mentored, you'll benefit by learning from somebody's wisdom so you'll be able to work smarter instead of harder.
- A mentor should never be dropped into a giant bottle of Diet Coke. (Oh wait, never mind. That's a Mentos.)

a mentor to Silas and Timothy. They mentored other people as well. (Paul even wrote a couple of books of the Bible to Timothy.)

Eventually we should all aim to follow Paul's example of being mentored and then mentoring others. In this way we'll build our lives into a beautiful puzzle and help others put together their puzzles as well.

God's Guide

Read: 1 Corinthians 11:1

1. Why do you think the apostle Paul told us to imitate him? What did he do that was worth imitating?

   _____

   _____

   _____

   _____

2. Who are some people in your life who "imitate Christ" that you could learn from? Write down a few names and the characteristics you appreciate about them. Which one would be the best mentor?

   _____

   _____

   _____

   _____

BONUS ACTIVITY

Line up a bunch of dominoes and knock them down. You can see some really cool videos of falling dominoes on the Internet. Just make sure to watch with your parents. Then set up and knock down other items. Books work well . . . cats, not so much.

The Great Debate

This was it. My school's debate team had a 10-point lead. All I had to do was make my speech. I looked the judges in the eyes to show confidence as I walked up to the microphone.

Boom!

Turns out, looking at the judges and not at the microphone was a bad idea. I smacked into the microphone with my forehead.

"Just wanted to start things off with a laugh," I said, hiding my embarrassment. "Now, when the judges stop laughing, I will. Uh . . . okay, I can wait a bit longer."

I stood at the mic for what seemed like an eternity. The judges finally calmed down, and it was time for me to win the debate for our team. The topic was "Is text messaging ruining the English language?"

The other team argued that kids didn't know how to spell correctly thanks to text messages. They said we just rely on AutoCorrect (Wow, I wasn't sure if that was one word or two. Thanks AutoCorrect!) to fix our spelling for us. They also said we used shortcuts. Instead of spelling out words like *what*, we short-ened it to *wut*. Yeah, wutever.

Our side argued the opposite point of view. Randy, our team captain, made a great point that kids were smart enough to know when to use proper spelling and when to be more casual. He pointed out that shortcut words were useful when sending a quick text. I texted him a smiley face when he finished to let him know how well he did.

So now it was my turn to make the closing arguments and win the debate! I tried to remember all the things my debate coach taught me. I knew I had to show confidence, but for some reason I was really nervous.

I cleared my throat. Unfortunately I was so nervous that my voice shot up four octaves. A high-pitched "Ahem" filled the room.

Where was my confidence? I've been talking since I was two years old! I talk in front of people all the time. I even make the morning announcements at school. Talking has never been a prob-lem for me . . . and I know many of my teachers would agree.

I steadied the microphone with my hand and looked around the room to see what was making that rattling sound. I quickly realized it was me. My shaking hand made the mic rumble in its stand like a roller coaster at Henry Hippo's Theme Park. I was not off to a good start.

Then I remembered my debate coach said to take a small sip of water if I was nervous. I reached for my water glass to take a sip. Big mistake!

All the ice somehow clung to the bottom of the glass until the very last second. Then it rushed forward without warning and splashed all over my face.

"Refreshing." I smiled.

The judges laughed again, which surprisingly gave me a little confidence. I started thinking about how God made me. He made me with a purpose. He had given me a voice to use and an ability to overcome embarrassment.

Feeling my confidence build, I started thinking about all my blessings. I have great parents and good friends. I live in a free country. I'm healthy.

Then I thought about all the ways God uses me to help people. I help Mrs. Fox take out her trash. I help my parents around the house! I help other people by telling them about Jesus!

As I stood there thinking, it suddenly hit me that I was supposed to be debating! I won't write everything I said in my final

Did You Know?

- More and more college students label themselves as "gifted" in writing ability, even though their test scores have actually gone down.
- Experts say that self-control is a much more powerful factor in personal success than self-esteem or self-confidence.
- It's possible to be confident and humble at the same time. It's called being "conhumblent."*

*You may want to check a dictionary before believing everything you read.

statements. But I did notice I was being filmed, so I'm pretty sure it will be on Netflix or at Redbox in a few months.

I had found my confidence, and (spoiler alert) we won the debate! Sorry for giving away the ending.

Confidence is a strange thing. God wants us to be confident yet humble. This used to confuse me. Then I realized that God wants us to be confident in Him! He created us with a plan and a purpose. We shouldn't let nerves stand in our way.

So if you're ever nervous, just keep in mind that you are a child of the King! You are made for greatness. And always remember to order your water without ice before a debate tournament.

Super Average Advice

Here's a quick question:

Who would say something like this? "I'm awesome! Look at me. Nobody's better. Bask in the greatness that is me."

a. a very confident person
b. a very narcissistic person
c. a professional football player after scoring a touchdown
d. all the above

Obviously the answer is *d*. However, *a* and *b* would probably do a lot less chest thumping.

We all need a certain amount of confidence in ourselves. Confidence is a good thing, but too much confidence can get ugly.

When you compete in anything—whether it's sports, debate, dance, or full-contact flute playing—you need to have confidence to do your best. If you're scared and timid, your God-given gifts won't be able to shine.

So how can you be confident without getting overconfident? Try these two things:

1. Look to the Lord. Many times the Bible tells us that God opposes the proud. Pride is a feeling that comes when we believe in our own abilities and achievements. But the truth is we wouldn't have any ability to achieve without God's blessing. When we miss that truth, that's bad news. As Proverbs 16:18 says, "Pride comes before destruction, and an arrogant spirit before a fall."

And then there's this verse in Jeremiah 17:7, where the prophet reminds us that "the man who trusts in the LORD, whose confidence indeed is the LORD, is blessed." What sounds better, destruction or blessing? Easy question, right?

2. Remember that you're a work in progress. You're going to make mistakes in life. Just because you know the Lord and have His Spirit living in you doesn't mean you're going to stop sinning. You're still going to battle pride. When we score a game-winning goal, make a victory-clinching speech, or ace a test, it's natural to think our abilities made the difference. But we never would've been in that position without God. So even then, He deserves the glory, not us.

Instead of getting overconfident, believe this: "I am confident of this very thing, that He who began a good work in you will perfect it until the day of Christ Jesus" (Philippians 1:6, NASB). God's not done with you yet. As you become more like Him, you'll get better and better each day. And that's a great way to build your confidence.

God's Guide

Read: Psalm 71:5–6

1. These verses talk about hope and confidence. Do you think these two things are related? How?

   _____

   _____

   _____

2. What does it mean to rely on the Lord? How can that give you confidence?

   _____

   _____

   _____

BONUS ACTIVITY

Get some friends and a tray of ice. Have everybody go outside, look up, and balance an ice cube on their foreheads. See who can keep it on the longest! (Note: Don't play this game in Minnesota in the winter—it'll go on forever!)

Super Average Garageless Sale

"You're late again, Pat," my teacher said.

Pat had shown up late for school again. If you haven't read my first book, you may not know who Pat is. (Now you're probably asking yourself, *Why haven't I read the first book? What's wrong with me?* That's a good question you just brought up on your own and without my help. I'm sure you'll fix that.)

Anyway, Pat is one of the bigger kids in my class, with an even bigger heart. He really cares about people and is a Christian, like me. He even saved my life once. But I'll let you read about that in book one.

Sadly, some kids make fun of him because of his size. As Pat hurried to take his seat, Clint whispered, "You're breathing hard, Pat. Did you run ten feet or something?"

Clint and Clay laughed.

"Keep making fun of me, Clint, and I'll show you my feet," Pat replied. "You don't want to see the toe I call Mr. Gnarly Blacknail. You won't eat for a week!"

Now it was my turn to laugh. I asked Pat why he was late. He said he didn't have his bike anymore and had to walk to school. He couldn't leave until his brother got picked up for day care, which made him late every day.

"I'll stop and pick you up," I said, wishing I was wearing a cape. (Insert superhero music here.) "I've got pegs on the back of my bike."

The next morning I stopped at Pat's house. Pat came bounding out and hopped on the back pegs of my bike. Now don't get me wrong; I've always wanted to do a wheelie. I just wasn't ready to do one right then. My front tire shot up in the air, and I fell into Pat.

"Sorry," Pat said, standing up. "Maybe I'm too big to ride on the back."

We tried several things. I tied our backpacks on the front of my bike to hold it down. That didn't work. I moved my pegs to the front, but then I couldn't see where I was going. We both ended up being late to class that day.

On the way to school, I asked, "What happened to your bike?"

"A lady in our neighborhood got a job but didn't have a way to get there," he said. "I gave her my bike so she could get to work."

Hang on, I thought. *I'm supposed to be the superhero.*

Pat had done an amazing selfless deed! And it gave me a great idea on how to get him a new bike. Right after school, I made some calls and went down to our local newspaper.

"Bob, we aren't running an article about how you can do half a chin-up," the chief editor said as I walked in.

"I'm here for something else this time," I said. I told him what Pat had done. They ran the story the next day. Everyone was talking about it, and even Clint and Clay started being nice to Pat.

Then I took some money I'd been saving and ran an ad for my great idea. The following day everybody in my town read about a "Garageless Garage Sale" to help buy Pat a new bike.

My plan was for people to donate one item from their house that they didn't use. Everything would be collected at my church, which would then hold a garage sale. My youth leader was totally on board. Turns out, so was half the town. Pat's story had made a huge impression. People started showing up with items. Others just donated money.

Did You Know?

- In 2000, four-year-old cancer patient Alexandra Scott organized a lemonade stand to help find a cure for all children with cancer. Since that time Alex's Lemonade Stand Foundation has raised more than $65 million for cancer research.
- Studies show that volunteering to help others builds your self-confidence and makes you happier.
- When Cee Cee Creech heard about the devastating tornadoes in Joplin, Missouri, in 2011, she wanted to do something to help. Only eight years old at the time, Cee Cee started knitting elephants. People purchased her elephants, helping raise more than $10,000.

The next morning about 400 people came to shop. We raised over $900! Even I emptied my piggy bank and bought two new—well, new to me—bike helmets, some Rollerblades, and a thing called a Snuggie. You know, things I really needed.

Pat got a new bike! We donated the rest of the money to our church for letting us use its parking lot and helping out so much. My youth pastor insisted on reimbursing me for the ad I bought to get the sale started. He even declared it "Super Average Garageless Sale Day" and said he planned to repeat the sale once a year to give the money to people in need.

It felt so great to be creative in helping someone. In fact, Pat and I went swimming after church on Sunday. We planned to brainstorm other creative ways to help people. We were having a great time . . . until he took off his shoes and I met Mr. Gnarly Blacknail.

Super Average Advice

Zach Hunter was in middle school when he found out slavery wasn't something you just read about in history books. The problem continue today—in a big way! Instead of thinking there was nothing a seventh grader could do, he launched Loose Change to Loosen Chains (LC2LC) to make others aware of and raise money for the 27 million people caught in modern-day slavery. What started as a program at his school and church spread around the world.

Zach's goal was straightforward. He wanted to end modern-day slavery. Now in his 20s, Zach has written four books and speaks all over the world about putting faith into action to make a difference for God.

You may never start your own foundation or speak around the globe, although you can speak "around" a globe by visiting a library. But God can use you to change lives. Just follow some of Zach's advice.

Find your passion. Zach's heart breaks when he thinks about slavery. All of the money raised by LC2LC goes to pulling people out of horrible situations and helping them build new lives. Maybe you're excited about feeding the hungry, providing clean water, helping people learn job skills, giving families farm animals, supplying medical care, or teaching people about Jesus. See what God puts on your heart. Then research the problem, find out what organizations are engaged in fixing that issue, and discover how you can get involved.

Make some change. Once you know what you're passionate about, tell people about it. Do reports in school. Talk to your youth pastor. Write to your grandparents. Your excitement can be contagious. Before you know it, other people will join your cause. That's what happened with Zach. He started collecting coins at his church and school, and pretty soon people around the world were donating their change to break chains.

Will it happen overnight? Probably not. Will it be hard? Probably. But that's okay. When you work hard and make sacrifices to help others, it pleases God. Hebrews 13:16 (ESV) says, "Do not neglect to do good and to share what you have, for such sacrifices are pleasing to God."

So get out there and get involved in making the world a better place. You don't have to be a superhero to be somebody's hero.

God's Guide

Read: 1 John 3:17–18

1. According to these verses, if we see people in need and don't help them, what does that say about us?

   _____

   _____

   _____

2. What's better: to talk about helping people or to actually help them by your actions? Think of someone who needs your help, and then go do it.

   _____

   _____

   _____

   _____

BONUS ACTIVITY

Hold your own garage sale. Take everything you haven't used in a year and sell it. (Brothers and sisters don't count and rarely get bought. Plus, the price tag usually keeps falling off of them.)

Hangin' with High Schoolers

"What are you guys doing?" I asked.

"We were playing 'hide from the nerd,' but I guess we're not very good at it." Mike laughed.

Mike's in high school. He and some of his friends were hanging out at the rec center after school. I saw my chance to impress them.

"Want to hear a joke?" I said.

"Shouldn't you be coloring or playing Duck, Duck, Goose?" Mike said. "You know, with kids your own age?"

"Whatever!" I said. "I don't play those little kid games. I come here to work out. Did you hear about the half chin-up I did last week?" This was true, by the way. Both the chin-up and the fact that I hadn't played Duck, Duck, Goose in over a week.

"You should tell the newspaper about that," Mike said.

"Exactly!" I shouted. "But they didn't think it was a big enough story."

"I was being sarcastic," Mike said.

I really wanted the high school kids to accept me so I could be part of their group. Last week I even tried to dress like a high schooler. Mike wears sunglasses all the time, so I walked into our lunchroom wearing my sunglasses. I felt really cool . . . for about 18 seconds.

My sunglasses have the darkest lenses I could find. They work great in the glaring sun when I'm fishing. But in the dimly lit cafeteria, I couldn't see at all. I felt around and found a lunch tray on the end of a table. Then I started scooping mashed potatoes onto it.

"What are you doing?" Karen yelled, running over to me. "That's my Styrofoam board with my bug collection on it!"

I pulled off my sunglasses to see 50 tiny bugs covered in a white, soupy mashed potato mess.

"Hmm, I bet the bugs will improve the taste of these mashed potatoes!" I joked.

I don't know why girls refuse to laugh out loud. That was a great joke, but Karen didn't even crack a smile. Anyway, the sunglasses thing didn't work out. Neither did the other things I tried.

The high schoolers all started wearing homemade armbands made from torn T-shirts with words printed on them. I'm not allowed to cut up my shirts, so I found a really thick rubber band in my dad's office. I wrote "Average Boy" on it and put it around my bicep (or where I thought my bicep would be if I had one).

This lasted about an hour. In math class, my teacher asked me to solve a problem on the board. I walked up and reached for the marker, only to discover the rubber band had cut off circulation in my arm. I couldn't move it at all!

"Is my class so dull that your arm fell asleep?" my teacher asked.

"No. My arm's trying out for the part of a noodle in the school play," I said. "It's getting into character."

I took off the rubber band and answered the problem using my left hand. It looked pretty good; however, my teacher asked if a small earthquake had been going off just under my feet when I was writing.

I wanted to reply with something funny, but my right arm decided to wake up at that precise moment. It felt like 200 ants stinging me. I started spinning around the room going "Auuughhhhh!" Not exactly the cool look I was going for.

In order to fit in, you're supposed to act like everyone else . . . which is hard. Still, I was determined to make the older kids like me. So there I was in the rec center, trying to fit in.

"Come on," I said. "Let me hang out with you guys."

"Okay," Mike said. "Tell us that joke."

This was my chance! All I had to do was say something funny.

"Uh, well. You see, uh . . ."

My brain froze up. I couldn't think of one funny thing. Thank goodness, at that exact moment, a basketball hit me in the head. (Now that's a sentence I never thought I'd write.) The ball bounced off my head as my eyes did a complete circle in their sockets. I wobbled a bit and collapsed to the floor. Laughter filled the room.

"Okay, that was pretty funny," Mike said. "You can hang out with us if you'll go buy us each a Coke."

I slowly stood up and reached into my pocket. I didn't have that kind of money. That's when it dawned on me. They didn't really want me to hang out with them. They just wanted to use me to get a free Coke.

I thought, *What am I doing? Why do I want these older kids to like me, when we really don't have anything in common?*

I guess everyone wants to be popular. But if it comes at a cost, it's not worth paying.

"No, thanks," I finally said. "I'm going to go see if my real friends want to play Duck, Duck, Goose."

Super Average Advice

Brock couldn't wait for the church retreat to begin. He'd arrived at the hotel the night before with his youth group. Thousands of Christian kids would be at the conference.

Did You Know?

- When you apply pressure to a spot on your arm or leg for a long period of time, you can cut off communication between it and your brain. When the nerves can't communicate, that part of your body goes to sleep.
- The largest game of Duck, Duck, Goose was played by 2,135 people at Logan-Rogersville High School in Rogersville, Missouri, in 2011.
- Some people wear sunglasses indoors to combat photophobia, a condition that makes them hypersensitive to light.

As Brock finished getting ready in the morning, he found a plastic shower cap, blew some air into it, and put it on his head.

"You look ridiculous," his youth leader said at breakfast.

Brock knew it looked funny, but he didn't care. He liked standing out as an individual. He went to all the teaching sessions, concerts, and meals with the shower cap on his head.

The next day when Brock and his friends walked to the first session, they were shocked to see hundreds of guys wearing plastic shower caps on their heads.

"Hey, you're a trendsetter," Brock's youth leader said.

As silly as it sounds, wearing a shower cap for a hat wouldn't even rank in the top 50 of wacky fads. From weird clothing styles to dangerous diets, people seem willing to do nearly anything to fit in.

- In the 1970s, bell-bottom jeans had openings at the legs almost as large as the opening at the waist.
- Sagging jeans gained popularity in the late 1990s, as people would buy huge jeans and "sag" them below their hips to show off much of their underwear.
- In the early 1900s, people ate tapeworm eggs hoping to lose weight. The parasite would grow in their stomachs, eating whatever they ate. To say this is dangerous is an understatement, but it's still being done today.

Have you ever wondered why people go to such great lengths to fit in? Isn't it easier—and better—to just be yourself? God created you with wonderful talents and abilities that He wants you to develop. When you go against your personality to fit into a group, you're not being the person God made you to be.

Sure, some trends aren't bad for you. Wearing SillyBandz won't make you a juvenile delinquent. But you need to know who you are and *whose* you are. When you understand that you're a child of the King of Kings, you'll be able to stand your ground instead of following what's cool at the time. Because some fads, such as drinking alcohol, huffing, and trying drugs, can be extremely dangerous.

Exodus 23:2 (NIrV) reminds us, "Do not follow the crowd when they do what is wrong." That's good advice. So is this: Bugs do not improve the taste of mashed potatoes!

God's Guide

Read: John 15:18–19

1. These verses seem to be saying that you're not going to fit into this world. How does that make you feel?

   _____

   _____

   _____

2. If your words and actions make you blend in with the kids around you, what should that tell you? Does God want you fitting in or standing out? Why?

   _____

   _____

   _____

BONUS ACTIVITY

Next time your mom makes mashed potatoes, have a contest with your family to see who can sculpt the coolest snowman.

A Great Goal

I scored a goal in soccer! It was awesome. This is my first year to play, but I'm obviously a natural.

Here's what happened. I was running around the field totally caught up in the game. I was also chasing a grasshopper. That's when I looked over and saw a kid climb on my bike and ride away. (Later I remembered that my parents had driven me to the game, so it just *looked* like my bike—which was at home in the garage.)

Anyway, when I stopped to watch him, the soccer ball hit me in the back of the head. I was caught off guard, but being the great athlete I am, I somehow directed the ball off my head and into the net.

It just shows that if you stay totally focused on the game, you will succeed. My coach later told me it was the winning goal. So I guess I scored my first goal *and* won the game!

The crowd cheered like crazy when the ball sailed into the net. Well, half of the crowd. The fans for my team weren't too happy. Turns out I didn't score for my team. Fans from the other team picked me up on their shoulders and carried me around the field.

This was a good thing, because several of my teammates were starting to chase me. Sitting up high kept me out of reach . . . except from Donny, who was able to hit me with his shoe.

After everyone calmed down and a few parents left (I'm guessing they were headed to anger-management classes), Coach had a talk with my team. He explained that I couldn't help being who I was.

This speech really embarrassed me. The coach shouldn't brag about me being such a great athlete. The talk worked, and my team decided to be friends with me again. Donny was the first to apologize.

"I'm sorry," he said. "Now can I have my shoe back?"

The rest of my teammates were so forgiving that they gave me a cool nickname: Benedict Arnold! I don't know much about Benedict Arnold, but I'm guessing he was a famous soccer player.

With soccer going so well, I decided I wanted to do another sport that used my feet, so I signed up for kung fu. My dad was

Did You Know?

- According to FIFA (International Federation of Football Association), the governing body of soccer, more than 265 million people play the sport around the world.
- In top professional soccer leagues, scoring goals can be difficult. Statistics show fewer than two goals are scored each game.
- The term *own goal* is used to describe when a player scores in his own net for the opposing team. The professional player record for lifetime own goals is nine.

hesitant to pay for the lessons, but I told him it'd teach me self-discipline, coordination, and persistence.

"Remember karate?" my dad said. "You quit after one class."

"I can't help that my feet are ticklish," I said. "Plus, if I'd taken kung fu first, I'd have learned about persistence and wouldn't have quit."

Last week I took my first couple of lessons. I like kung fu because you get to wear pajamas and break things without getting in trouble. You also have to answer the teacher with "Yes, sir."

If you forget, you have to do 10 push-ups. I already answer adults with "Yes, sir," so I never have to do any push-ups.

In my second class, we worked on breaking boards. I don't like to brag, but I broke my board in only 203 punches.

"Come on," my teacher said. "Look at Kelsey. She broke her board in only one hit!"

"Yes, sir," I said. "Some people are just lazy and try to get things over with really fast."

Every year I try something new. This year it's soccer and kung fu. Last year I did archery and waterskiing. Neither lasted long, but at least I tried something new.

I would have stuck with archery, but unfortunately my bow was broken in a freak accident that involved a tornado coming through our house while I was at school, and only my dad was home. Oddly enough, the tornado only broke my bow and blew away the mouthpiece to my brother's trumpet. Everything else in the garage was unharmed.

Anyway, the point is: God gives us each day, and we need to use it to the fullest. So try something new today. Find a new activity. If you work hard at it, maybe you'll be the next Benedict Arnold.

Super Average Advice

Each day is precious. In Psalm 90:12, Moses wrote, "Teach us to number our days carefully so that we may develop wisdom in our hearts." By numbering your days and understanding that life is a wonderful God-given adventure, you grow wise. And one of the wisest ways you can use your time is by trying new activities.

A popular quote says, "Don't fear failure so much that you refuse to try new things. The saddest summary of a life contains three descriptions: could have, might have, and should have." Trying new things makes life exciting and new—and God is a God of newness. Isaiah 43:19 (ESV) says, "Behold, I am doing a new thing; now it springs forth, do you not perceive it? I will make a way in the wilderness and rivers in the desert."

When you try a new endeavor, you benefit yourself in many ways.

You build courage. It takes courage to step out and tackle a new activity. You have skills to learn, people to meet, and decisions to make. The more courage you show now, the easier it is to act courageously in the future.

You see the possibilities. If you're not willing to try something new, you might miss out on finding one of your passions or making an amazing discovery. Just think if a Mayan Indian hadn't been willing to try this weird new drink made from water and crushed cocoa beans, then hot chocolate might never have been discovered! Being willing to take a risk can result in something great . . . not to mention delicious. When you experiment with various activities, you're bound to find an area where you naturally excel.

You bust boredom. It's hard to get bored when you're constantly trying something new. Your brain was designed to conquer challenges and learn new things. Keep your brain engaged by attempting different activities.

Now's the perfect time to learn something new. As you go through middle school and high school, take advantage of opportunities to expand your knowledge and break out of your comfort zone. Take a photography class. Learn how to edit videos. Pick up a second—or even third—language. Go out for a sport you've never played before.

At first it can feel scary to take a risk. But you don't want to look back later in life and say, "I could've been a good soccer player," or "I should've gone out for the school play."

Because that would just be sad.

God's Guide

Read: Ephesians 4:22–24

1. What do you think it means to "put on the new self"? How is your new self different from the old self?

   _____

   _____

   _____

2. God wants us to act differently and try new things with the new life He's given us. Write down some things you'd like to do that could bring glory to God.

_____

_____

_____

BONUS ACTIVITY

Count how many times you can "juggle" a soccer ball by keeping it in the air using only your feet, knees, and head. World-record holder Nikolai Kutsenko juggled a soccer ball for more than 24 hours straight!

Cutting It Close

I was going to be late. Mom said to be home by eight o'clock so I could watch my brother while she went to a meeting at church. I thought about pretending I didn't know whether she meant a.m. or p.m. But I knew that was lying. Plus, I knew it wouldn't work.

I was at Billy's house watching a movie called *Samson and the Super Cut Special*. A better title would've been *The Movie That's Way Too Long to Watch If You Have a Curfew*. I kept looking at my watch. I don't know why I do that. My watch quit working right after I hit that tree with my bike. I'd still like to know who planted that tree right in the middle of the forest! Anyway, the clock in Billy's living room told me I had 15 minutes before I had to be home.

"How much longer till this is over?" I asked.

"Probably 15 more minutes," Billy said. "You've read the Bible story. You know how it ends. If you have to go, just go."

I loved Samson's story. At first I thought God put it in the Bible to remind us that girls can be trouble—especially if they own scissors! But now I realize that Samson's life teaches us to stick to God's rules and not be deceived by others.

I made a decision. I had to go. Unfortunately I made this decision 10 minutes later . . . when the movie finally ended. I sped outside to get my bike with only five minutes to spare. However, a spare was what I needed. My bike had a flat tire!

Billy's bike was still broken from our latest invention. The "slingshot bike" still had some kinks to be worked out. But I didn't have time to think about that now.

Normally it took me 15 minutes to bike to Billy's house. But I figured I was in great shape, so I could probably run it in five. I took off sprinting. I ran for a long time. With my watch broken, I had no idea how long I'd been running when Mrs. Fox pulled up in her car at the top of Billy's driveway.

"Need a lift?" She smiled.

"Yeah, I need to get home right away," I said. "I'm late!"

"Climb in," Mrs. Fox said, still smiling. "This car is built for speed!"

Now if you don't read my *Adventures in Odyssey Clubhouse* magazine articles, you may not know my neighbor Mrs. Fox. She's really funny and really old. We're always helping each other out. I jumped into the car, and she slowly crept back on the road at about six miles an hour.

"Can we go any faster?" I asked.

"Sure," she said, not going any faster.

"Why aren't we going faster?" I asked.

"Oh, I thought you just wanted to know if we could go any faster." She laughed.

She picked up speed, but it still took us forever to get home. We finally pulled into my driveway at 8:22 p.m. As soon as I climbed out of the car and thanked Mrs. Fox, she peeled out of my driveway going super fast. I ran inside and saw my mom.

"I'm here!" I said. "You can go to your meeting."

"It's too late," she said. "I won't get there in time."

I felt horrible. Mom had been looking forward to hanging out with her friends. I didn't know what to say, which for me is a big deal.

"I'm sorry, Mom. It won't happen again."

"Oh, I know. Kids who have to write 100 sentences about why they won't be late usually are never late again."

It was a good reminder. Grown-ups give curfews and rules for a reason. And just like Samson, I need to follow the rules I'm given. I went to get a pencil and paper and then stopped.

"Instead of sentences, couldn't you just cut my hair?"

Super Average Advice

For most kids, their goal in life is to have maximum fun with minimum discomfort. King Solomon, one of the wisest men to ever live, sort of agreed. In Ecclesiastes 8:15, he wrote, "So I commended enjoyment because there is nothing better for man under the sun than to eat, drink, and enjoy himself." God wants us to have fun and enjoy life.

Of course, if you totally devote yourself to having fun, you may

Did You Know?

- By the time children reach fifth grade, 80 percent of them have been spanked or received physical punishment from a parent.
- When two young brothers damaged their family's bathtub in a Beyblade battle, their mom sold their toys on eBay to help pay for the $500 repair. She ended up making $9,000!*
- Writing sentences as punishment may have started in schools. Other popular school punishments from the past include wearing a dunce cap, standing in the corner while facing the wall, sitting on a high stool next to the teacher's desk, and standing while holding a heavy book at arm's length.

*No, this wasn't Average Boy and his brother.

end up living a very self-centered and shallow existence. It's not fun if your enjoyment leads to another person missing out or feeling bad.

As a follower of God, your goal in life should be to become more like Jesus—not just to have fun. Parents have the same goal for their children, which is why they put rules in place. Rules aren't created to ruin fun. Rules enhance fun by keeping you safe and making you responsible to the people around you.

So instead of pushing the boundaries of your family's rules (which can often get you in trouble), think about these ideas:

Following rules equals love. If you want to show God you love Him, what do you do? The apostle John had the answer. In 1 John 5:3, he wrote, "This is what love for God is: to keep His commands." By following God's rules, we show Him that we love Him. The same thing is true for our parents. When we follow their rules, it shows how much we love and care for them.

Love discipline. How can you love something that's painful? Because let's face it, discipline equals discomfort. None of us love to be grounded or have our cell phones taken away. Instead of loving discipline, we usually just endure it until it's over so we can get back to regular life.

But wise King Solomon said, "Whoever loves discipline loves knowledge, but one who hates correction is stupid" (Proverbs 12:1, NIV). Did he just say stupid? Some kids get in trouble for just saying that word. But Solomon wanted to make his point: If you don't like being corrected, then that's stupid. So be smart and embrace discipline. Learn from it. And try not to make the same mistakes again . . . especially when it comes to haircuts.

God's Guide

Read: Hebrews 12:11

1. What's the toughest discipline you've ever received from your parents? What did you learn from it?

   _____

   _____

   _____

2. How do you usually respond to being disciplined? Does it make you angry? Do you just deal with it? What do you think it means to be trained by discipline?

   _____

   _____

   _____

BONUS QUESTION

What is your favorite feat that Samson performed? (Killing 1,000 Philistines with the jawbone of a donkey was pretty impressive.)

EXTRA BONUS QUESTION

If you have some free time, go online and bid on my Beyblades!

Comedic Calling

i love being a kid for a lot of reasons:

1. I can sneeze into my sleeve. (For some reason this really grosses out grown-ups.)
2. I can misuse words, such as *inelephantly*, and people think it's cute.
3. I don't have to worry about paying taxes every year.
4. Food magically appears in the refrigerator. Then I do a trick where I make it disappear.

Yup, being a kid is awesome! Even the few chores I do are nothing compared to what my mom does.

I learned that lesson when my dad started Mom Appreciation Day. My dad came up with this new holiday when I walked into the living room and said, "Mom, this shirt needs washing."

"Please, will you wash this shirt?" my dad quickly said.

"Oh, I guess Dad has a shirt he wants washed too," I added.

Dad shook his head and looked at me. He informed me that he

was showing me how to ask properly. Then I said the worst thing you can say about your mom.

"But that's what she does."

Thus was born Mom Appreciation Day! For one day I had to do all the things Mom does around the house. It was horrible. I never worked so hard in my life! I finally collapsed on the couch . . . too tired to even eat.

My dad walked into the living room and said I needed to come to the table and eat dinner so I could get my energy back.

I learned an important lesson that day about how hard grown-ups work. But it also made me think, *What do I want to do when I grow up?*

I knew I wanted a wife and kids, so I knew I'd need a job. But really, what was I going to do with my life?

That's a question we should all ask ourselves. Then I thought of a better question: *What does God want me to do with my life?*

Did You Know?

- When a group of five-year-olds in New York City was asked what they wanted to be when they grew up, the top answers were (1) superhero, (2) firefighter, (3) princess, and (4) police officer.
- Mother's Day became an official United States holiday in 1914.
- According to *U.S. News & World Report*, the best jobs in 2013 were dentist, registered nurse, pharmacist, computer systems analyst, and physician.

I started asking all the grown-ups I knew what they thought God wanted me to be.

Mrs. Fox said I could be a fireman. She reminded me how quickly I put out the fire I started in her backyard.

Billy's dad said I could be a construction worker. He said I was really good at rebuilding their fence after all those times Billy and I accidentally knocked it down.

My teacher said I could be a comedian. She even encouraged me to work on it right away. "Quit school," she said. "I'll write you a hall pass. Leave right now and make my dreams . . . uh, your dreams come true!"

She was joking, but she had a point. Maybe I could be a Christian comedian. I could make people laugh and then tell them about Jesus. Laughter is a powerful tool, and I'd already seen God use my abilities.

Last year I was sitting next to this lady at church who was crying. I didn't know her, but I could tell she was really sad. I decided to cheer her up.

I have two go-to moves that always make people laugh. The first involves my eyebrows. I can mash up my forehead and push my eyebrows together to create the letter M. The second thing I do is play the song "Amazing Grace." This usually gets a laugh because I play it using my hand and armpit.

I decided to go with the M idea. I leaned over, squished together my eyebrows, and said, "Excuse me, lady, I know you're sad. But my eyebrows want you to know that things will get mmmmuch, mmmuch better!"

She looked over, still crying, and said, "What? AHAAAA HAAAAAAAA!"

Laughter filled the room. Joy instantly filled her heart. I'd never heard laughter that loud before. It was awesome. Well, I thought it was awesome. The rest of the people at the funeral didn't think it was that great. I saved the day, though, with a fantastic and heartfelt solo of "Amazing Grace"!

Anyway, that's my plan. I'm going to be a Christian comedian so I can spread happiness and tell people about God!

But I knew I could start spreading happiness right away. I began with my mom. Giving her a hug, I said, "Mom, you're awesome. I appreciate all you do for me."

She hugged me tightly. Then with a tear in her eye, she handed me a shirt and told me to wash it for her.

Super Average Advice

Finding God's will is like riding a bike. Once you figure it out, you never forget how to do it. At least, that's what Phil Vischer, the co-creator of VeggieTales and the voice of Bob the Tomato, says. (The riding-the-bike part, not the forgetting part.)

Phil said to picture your life as if you're riding a tandem bi-cycle. Your natural inclination is to sit up front so you can steer. Bad idea, because you're not really sure where you're going. Instead, you need to let Jesus take the handlebars. (*Hmmm*, that's kind of catchy.) Your job is to pedal and let God direct where you're going. Phil says you'll never find God's will sitting on the couch. You have

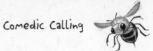

to actively follow God and work on developing your talents. When you pedal hard and allow God to guide you, you'll be on the right path.

But sometimes we want to know for sure that we're on the right path. Wouldn't it be nice if God talked to us like He did Moses?

Moses: Whoa! Look at that burning bush.

God: I am the God of your father.

Moses: Okay, the bush is talking. I must've been tending these sheep too long.

God: I am sending you to Pharaoh so that you may lead My people, the Israelites, out of Egypt.

Moses: Are you sure about that?

God: Did I stutter?

All right, maybe the conversation sounded a little different (you can read the whole thing in Exodus 3:1–17). But at the end of their talk, Moses knew exactly what God wanted him to do.

As followers of Jesus, we want the same certainty of knowing God's plan for our lives. He may not talk too much anymore through blazing shrubs, but God still speaks to us through His Word, His church, His Spirit, His people, and circumstances He puts in our lives.

As you seek God's will, remember to read your Bible. He'll guide you through different stories and verses. A great verse can be found in 1 Peter 2:15: "It is God's will that you silence the ignorance of foolish people by doing good."

Doing good is always part of God's plan for your life. In addition, He wants you to listen to the people He puts around you, such as parents, teachers, pastors, and older family members. They may see a talent in you that you hadn't noticed.

Being open and sensitive to God's leading will keep you in His will. And always remember the words of a famous tomato: "God made you special, and He loves you very much."

God's Guide

Read: Proverbs 3:5–6

1. What do you do more often—trust in God or rely on yourself? Be honest. Why did you answer that way?

   _____

   _____

   _____

2. Why is it important to stay on the right path? How can thinking about God help you find the path He wants you on?

   _____

   _____

   _____

BONUS ACTIVITY

Be a Christian comedian one night! Go to *Godtube.com* and search for "Bob Smiley." Watch a few videos, write a joke or two yourself, and then get in front of your family to perform.

Dress to Impress

Your jeans have holes in them!" my mom said.

"Of course they have holes in them," I joked. "That's how I get my legs in."

Sometimes my jokes cause my mom to launch into a monologue. She made a 10-minute speech about how it was important to look my best.

That's when I remembered a great idea from an awards show I'd watched the previous night. If one of the winners talked too long, the band started playing music, which meant it was time to wrap up the speech.

So while I listened to my mom, I walked over and grabbed my trombone. I started playing the only song I knew—the theme music to a movie called *Jaws*. My dad says with the way I play the song, it's actually scarier than the movie.

"What are you doing?" Mom said.

"We're running short on time, so I'm playing a song to let you know it's time to wrap it up."

My song quickly came to an end, because my mom walked over and stuffed a sock into the end of my trombone.

Once I thought about it, I knew she was right . . . as always. We were headed to church. I show God respect when I look my best to worship Him. Five minutes later, I came back dressed in nice pants, a shirt, and a tie.

Before we left, Mom adjusted the tie around my neck. I had it on my head like a headband. (I guess that look hasn't caught on at church yet.)

"I see you combed your hair," she said, laughing.

"How'd you know?" I asked.

"The comb's still stuck in the back of that nest you call a hair style."

So that's where my comb went! I thought. I had been combing my hair when my favorite song came on the radio. I stopped to sing along and couldn't find where I laid down my comb when it was over.

Anyway, we headed off to church. As I walked in, I was in-

Did You Know?

- The tradition of dressing up for church began in England in the 1800s. Before that, only the rich could afford fancy clothes.
- When you dress up for church, some people call it "putting on your Sunday best."
- Ripped jeans used to be a sign of poverty. Then they became a symbol of rebelliousness. Now they're just sort of ho-hum.

stantly complimented by the greeter on how good I looked. Then I started to notice how other kids were dressed. Several boys wore jeans . . . sort of. Their belts and pants were hanging around their thighs. Baggy pants have been popular, but I've never been into that. For starters, what if you're playing tag. You can't run with your pants holding your legs together!

Other guys wore pants so tight that they gripped their legs like a pair of leggings. Not a great look.

The girls weren't dressed any better. Some of their clothes were pretty tight too. My dad and I have talked about this a lot. Dressing a certain way can cause guys to look at girls differently.

You see, my dad taught me that it's important to guard my eyes and my heart. I shouldn't look at things that cause bad thoughts in my brain. At first I thought he was talking about math. (I always have bad thoughts when I stare at a math book.) But he was talking about staying pure in my mind and heart. We shouldn't allow anything into our brains that will cause us to stumble.

So not only is it important to dress for the occasion; it's also important to dress modestly, because you never know who you are causing to stumble. Some girls at my church needed to learn that lesson. Thankfully, I knew what to do. I pulled my tie up over my eyes and asked my mom to lead me past temptation.

Super Average Advice

Where does beauty come from? How about masculinity?

If you believe what you see in advertisements, you can become attractive by purchasing the right jeans, shirt, shampoo, or perfume.

Flip open a magazine, turn on the TV, watch a movie, or search the Internet, and you'll come face-to-face with models and actors who appear to have lost some of their clothes or purchased something too small and tight—all in the name of beauty.

The Bible paints a very different picture. First Peter 3:3–4 says, "Your beauty should not consist of outward things like elaborate hairstyles and the wearing of gold ornaments or fine clothes. Instead, it should consist of what is inside the heart with the imperishable quality of a gentle and quiet spirit, which is very valuable in God's eyes." Instead of outward beauty, God wants us to concentrate on beauty that comes from the heart.

Fashions fade. Clothing styles change. But your heart goes with you everywhere you go. (At least it better; otherwise you're a medical marvel!) By working on having a beautiful heart, you'll draw the right people to you—and more important, you'll draw them to God.

Being fashionable and looking good isn't necessarily bad. If you battle with your parents about what you wear, that's bad. Clothing can bring out your personality. But compromising your character by making poor clothing choices isn't a good idea.

First Timothy 2:9 says, "Women are to dress themselves in modest clothing, with decency and good sense." Modesty, decency, and good sense—that's a winning wardrobe combination we should all try to follow.

Now you've probably noticed that most Bible verses about

clothing relate to women. If you're a girl, you might be thinking, *Hey, that's not fair!* And you're right. It's not fair. But it's a fact that how you dress will affect how boys look at you. So make sure they see the real you—a daughter of the King . . . a princess!

As you decide what to wear every morning, try to block out the messages from the media (and probably some of your friends). Listen to God's Word about true beauty and make a fashion statement.

Just make sure that statement is "I'm a follower of Jesus Christ."

God's Guide

Read: 1 Corinthians 10:31

1. If what you eat and drink should bring glory to God, how do you think God wants you to dress?

   _____

   _____

   _____

   _____

2. How can you glorify God with what you wear? Should your clothes draw attention to you? If so, what kind of attention?

   _____

   _____

   _____

   _____

BONUS ACTIVITY

Go through your parents' high school yearbooks and try to re-create their hairstyles and wardrobes. See if they notice which of them you're dressed as when you go to dinner that night.

Knock, Knock

Our church recently completed a door-knocking campaign. We knocked on neighbors' doors and told them about Jesus. This was definitely a job for a superhero! Since my neighbors all live on farms, I had to get up really, really early on Saturday morning.

My alarm went off at 10:30 a.m.

At first I couldn't remember why I was getting up so early. Then my super memory kicked in, and I thought about how the apostle Paul suffered in chains for Christ. If Paul could do it, so could I! I crawled out of bed and was on my bike by 11:45.

Twenty minutes later, I came back home. Mrs. Ray, our closest neighbor, said she would talk to me after I brushed my teeth.

"Much better!" she said when I returned. "Now what have you got for me?"

I gathered my courage. "I want to tell you about Jesus."

"You did that at the fair two months ago," she reminded me. "I've been going to your church."

"So I brushed my teeth for nothing," I said.

"I wouldn't say that," she replied. "But how could you forget that I attend your church? I sat next to you and your parents last Sunday. The pastor was talking about Eve eating the apple. You turned to me and said that if Snow White had read the Bible, she wouldn't have made the same mistake."

"Oh yeah," I said. (My super memory obviously hadn't quite kicked in yet.)

As I walked away, I wasn't too discouraged. It's good to do a practice run before doing the real thing.

Next I knocked on Mr. Speck's door. He's a beekeeper. Mr. Speck is older than most of the trees on his farm. I like listening to his crazy stories about how things were before email . . . or running water.

He eventually opened the door and greeted me warmly: "Bob, you try this every month, but trick-or-treating only works once a year."

Did You Know?

- Four out of 10 people who attend church haven't shared their faith in Jesus with anybody in the last six months.
- Six out of 10 Americans don't know their neighbors' first names.
- More people admit to knowing the names of their neighbors' pets (27 percent) than the names of their neighbors' kids (24 percent).

"This time I want to tell you about Jesus," I said. "Hey, you might have actually gone to school with Him when you were a kid!"

I thought a joke might be a good icebreaker.

Mr. Speck smiled. "You and Billy did that last month. Billy now comes over once a week to read the Bible to me."

Still undaunted, I rode to the last three houses. Mr. and Mrs. Hines weren't home, but their TV was on. Through the door I heard a show playing where two people were talking in quiet voices.

"It's that crazy neighbor kid!" one voice said.

"Don't open the door," someone answered. "He's probably trying to get candy again."

It sounded like a good show, but missionaries can't get sidetracked, so I went to Mrs. Chaney's house. I was about to knock when I remembered that my parents do a Bible study with her. (See, my super memory *can* come in handy.)

So I went to the last house on my list, Mr. Polvado. He walked outside before I even knocked.

"Want to go fishing?" he asked.

"No, I came to tell you about Jesus."

"You talked to me and Mrs. Ray about Jesus at the church fair," he said. "She's really been after me to go to church. I guess I'll go next Sunday . . . if the fish aren't biting."

An hour later I pedaled home completely discouraged. My dad walked up and asked what was wrong.

"I got up early to do the door-knocking campaign," I explained.

"I was excited to tell our neighbors about Jesus, but everyone's already heard me talk about Him."

"Bob, are you disappointed that you've already been spreading the good news?" Dad said. "If I were you, I'd take that as a compliment. It just means you've been doing your job daily instead of waiting for a challenge."

I hadn't really thought about that. As God's ambassadors, we should talk about Him every day—not just during door-knocking campaigns. It's a constant thing. With that in mind, I grabbed my fishing pole and headed back to Mr. Polvado's house. If I'd already been a fisher of men, then maybe I could spend the rest of the day fishing for . . . well, fish.

Super Average Advice

Francis of Assisi is often quoted as saying, "Preach the gospel at all times; when necessary, use words." Many experts today doubt the powerful preacher ever uttered those words. Something else this famous monk probably never said is "A bird in the hand is better than two in my belly."

Whether or not Saint Francis said that phrase about the gospel during his lifetime nearly 900 years ago, it's still an interesting thought to ponder.

Your actions speak loudly about your faith in Christ. In John 13:35, Jesus said, "By this all people will know that you are My disciples, if you have love for one another." Your actions can demonstrate love clearly and powerfully. You can bring people closer to

Christ by showing them love. It's a good idea to "preach" to your friends about God's love and His good news through your actions. But when it comes to sharing the difference Jesus has made in your life, it's always necessary to use words.

Telling others about your faith in Christ can be scary. That's probably why a lot of people don't do it. They don't want to be rejected or feel awkward. Not everybody will agree with your beliefs, but that shouldn't stop you from sharing.

God wants us to preach the gospel and spread the good news about Him. It's our job as Christ's followers to take His message of grace around the world. And it's a message unique to the Christian faith. In John 14:6, Jesus said, "I am the way, the truth, and the life. No one comes to the Father except through Me."

Many religions claim to be right. But only Christianity holds these truths:

- You don't earn your way to eternal life. You can't get to heaven with your good deeds—only Jesus' amazingly sacrificial deed of dying on the cross makes it possible. We just need to believe.
- Jesus died and came back to life. He's the only God to do that.
- In other religions, people reach up to God, trying to become minigods. In Christianity, God reaches down to us to make us holy and righteous.

As you step out to share your faith, do it boldly. You have the truth on your side. You have God's love on your side. So share those things with your words *and* actions.

God's Guide

Read: Matthew 28:19–20

1. This portion of Scripture is called the Great Commission,
    where Jesus told His followers to make disciples. Who does
    Jesus want us to tell about Him?

    _____

    _____

    _____

2. Do you think Jesus helps give you the right things to say
    when you witness to others about Him? How do you know?
    What do you think Jesus meant in verse 20 when He said, "I
    am with you always"?

    _____

    _____

    _____

Bonus Activity

Talk to your parents about your faith in Christ and the difference He's made in your life. Then when you have an
opportunity to tell someone else about Jesus, you'll have
practiced what you want to say.

Down but Not Out

"Can I talk to you after practice?" my basketball coach said.

My heart sank. In my experience, that's never good news.

Of course I knew I was an important member of the team, because I'd do anything to help the team. Last week, for example, my coach was busy, so I washed the towels for him. I did this to be nice and in no way hoped he'd start me in the next game. Although I did leave him a note saying, "You can thank me at the beginning of our next game . . . unless I'm on the court."

Turns out, no thanks was needed. The school's dryer is way different from the one at my home. Our dryer barely dries clothes on high heat. But the "High Heat" setting on the school's dryer shrinks a towel to the size of a washcloth. I pointed out that the school wouldn't have to buy washcloths for a while, but my coach wasn't amused.

Maybe Coach wants to talk with me about the exploding basketball incident. I thought.

Yesterday I offered to air up the basketballs after practice. I wasn't strong enough to push down the bicycle pump that Coach normally uses. So I found Mr. Gribble, our school janitor, and asked him if I could borrow the air compressor. I hooked up the first ball to the compressor and turned on the air. That's when Wendy walked by.

"Watcha doing?" she asked.

"Well, as you know, I'm on the basketball team," I said, trying not to brag.

"Yeah, you've really kept that bench warm all season."

I started to laugh, but an explosion startled me and caused me to do two things:

1. Scream.

2. Jump into Wendy's arms.

We were practically face-to-face. Not knowing what to do, I just smiled.

"You've got broccoli in your teeth," she said.

"Yup! Athletes have to eat healthy."

Anyway, the coach might have wanted to talk to me about the loss of our best basketball. For the rest of practice, I couldn't concentrate. I missed every layup and dribbled the ball off my foot six times.

After practice I walked into Coach's office and apologized.

"I'm sorry I was so bad at practice today."

"I didn't notice any difference," he said.

Then my world crashed in.

"Bob, this weekend is the big tournament," Coach said. "I just found out we can only take ten players, and we have eleven on the team."

"Trent'll be so disappointed," I said. "Do you want me to tell him he's not going?"

But that wasn't my coach's plan. I'd been cut from the team. I walked out of the office not sure what to do next. I had to tell my parents. I knew Wendy would find out. I was embarrassed and disappointed. For the rest of the day, I was quiet.

Everyone noticed.

"You okay?" my science teacher said. "You haven't said or broken anything."

"I'm a little depressed," I told him. "Coach said I wasn't needed this weekend at the basketball tournament."

"Is the bench there self-heating?" he said. "Just joking. You know, everything happens for a reason. Maybe you'll be able to encourage someone in the future who's been disappointed, because you're going through this now. God works out everything for the good of those who love Him."

He had a good point. I left school a little more encouraged . . . until my dad got home.

"I have to tell you something," I said, my voice shaking.

"Okay, but get out of the massage chair first," Dad replied. "You sound strange when your voice shakes like that."

I told him what my coach said. Instead of being disappointed, he broke out in a smile.

"Hey, that's okay," he said. "I've been wanting to take you fishing, and the weather's going to be perfect tomorrow."

The next morning two things happened. First, I realized my dad knows nothing about the weather. The storm hit right as we arrived at the lake. And second, my dad doesn't let anything disappoint him. Instead of fishing, we called my mom. She and my brother swung by and picked up Wendy, and we all went to the movies.

Did You Know?

- Basketballs bounce well when they're inflated to around eight psi (pounds per square inch) of pressure. Balls explode at around 80 psi.
- Only one out of five kids participate in vigorous physical activity five or six days a week.
- Michael Jordan failed to make the varsity high school basketball team as a sophomore, while his taller friend made it. But Jordan didn't dwell on the disappointment. He went on to become one of the best basketball players in history!

That weekend I learned that if you truly have faith in God, disappointing news shouldn't ruin your day, your week, or your life. You can still be sad, but it shouldn't consume you.

After the movies, I even thanked Wendy for not making fun of me for getting cut from the team.

"You're a great friend," I said with a huge grin.

She smiled back and said, "Seriously? How much broccoli do you eat?!?"

Super Average Advice

Disappointment is part of life. Your team loses. You don't get picked for the solo in the choir. Your test doesn't go as well as you hoped. You're not invited to a classmate's birthday party.

Don't you feel better now?

No? That's understandable.

But also remember that sometimes you'll hit the game-winning shot, ace the test, earn the part, and go to the party. You've probably noticed it's easy to be happy when everything goes your way. The tricky part is maintaining your joy during disappointments.

Here's the truth: Disappointments hurt.

Here's a bigger truth: When you fail or suffer disappointment, it doesn't change how much God—or your family—loves you. God loves exactly the same the best big league baseball player and the kid who can't throw a ball two feet.

So when you suffer a disappointment, it's okay to be sad. But you shouldn't stay that way. Knowing that God loves you and that everything works together for good for those who love Him will allow you to turn your troubles into opportunities (Romans 8:28). If you get cut from the basketball team, you may be able to comfort a friend who doesn't make the school play.

Have you ever heard the saying, "When God closes a door, He opens a window"? At first that can sound like a huge waste of energy, especially if it's winter and all that heat goes out the window. But it means if one opportunity doesn't work out, you should look for where God is leading you.

No matter what happens, God doesn't want you to be troubled or dwell on past disappointments. John 14:27 says, "Peace I leave with you. My peace I give to you. I do not give to you as the world gives. Your heart must not be troubled or fearful."

By understanding God's peace, you'll be able to deal better with disappointment and look forward to future blessings. That's something to take to heart . . . and through that window.

God's Guide

Read: Romans 5:3–5

1. When you experience disappointment, do you naturally want to rejoice? Why not?

   _____

   _____

   _____

2. Why do these verses tell you to rejoice when afflictions come
   your way? What's the result when you persevere and learn
   from your difficulties?

   _____

   _____

   _____

BONUS ACTIVITY

Have a contest with your friends to see who can blow up a
balloon the fastest until it pops. Just make sure that your
friends know to stop blowing if they feel dizzy, and that
everyone around knows about the game. The popping
noise can scare people if they aren't expecting it. Trust me.
It took me forever to clean up the eggs my mom broke.

Sigh . . . Why Did I Lie?

Ever heard the phrase "Liar, liar, pants on fire"? Wouldn't it be cool if it actually happened! Imagine how easy it'd be to tell if someone was lying.

Teacher: Did you do your homework?

Student: Yes, I did all my hom—AUUGGGHHHHH! My pants are on fire! Someone grab a hose!

Teacher: Stop, drop, and roll! And then finish problems nine through fourteen.

Of course, some people might lie if they didn't like the pants they were wearing. My aunt once gave me a pair of plaid pants that looked like a clown threw up on my legs. I'd gladly tell a fib to make those things disappear!

Speaking of disappearing, two days ago Mom answered the phone.

"Hello, Karen," she said, immediately striking fear in my heart.

Karen and some other girls have been calling, trying to get me to come hang out with them. I've been able to avoid them so far with some clever excuses. I'd already used homework, chores, baby-sitting my brother, and the swine flu. I had to really sell the last one to make it believable. For a week I made oinking sounds to convince the girls I wasn't over my sickness yet.

So when I heard my mom on the phone with Karen, I quickly motioned that I wasn't home. My mom covered the phone and said, "Bob, you are here. I'm not going to lie."

I quickly ran outside and shut the door. I then mouthed, "Tell her I'm outside!"

My mom gave me a stern look but said, "He's outside right now. Can I take a message?"

She then broke into a big grin, which is never a good sign.

"What did she say?" I asked through the glass.

Did You Know?

- When Divertical opened to the public in June 2012, it became the world's tallest water ride. Located in Ravenna, Italy, this water coaster takes boats 197 feet into the air before plunging them into the water.
- Wisconsin Dells is known as the Waterpark Capital of the World! This tiny Wisconsin town boasts more than 20 indoor waterparks and numerous outdoor parks, including Noah's Ark—the largest outdoor waterpark in the United States.
- Wet 'n Wild in Orlando, Florida, opened in 1977, making it the first major waterpark in America.

"I'll tell you when you get home," she said, locking the back door. My mom has a strange sense of humor.

An hour later Mom opened the door and told me Karen had an extra ticket to Splash City.

"What?" I shouted. "I love Splash City! Why didn't you tell me?"

"You weren't home, remember?" she said.

I was so bummed. Splash City Waterpark has a ride called the Tower of Torture, which sounds like something that involves homework. It doesn't. It's actually a big tower with a ton of stairs. When you get to the top, you dodge low-flying airplanes until it's your turn to go down a big slide. (Or you can walk back down the stairs as my dad proved the last time we went.) They also have water guns for shooting water at people . . . until the workers make you stop.

The next day Karen said, "Sorry you missed Splash City! Wendy was looking forward to hearing you scream when you rode the Tower of Torture! I told her you'd probably oink the whole way down."

Okay. This was too much. Not only did I miss out on Splash City, but I missed out on hanging with Wendy! Plus, she probably thought I was sick. I had to set things right.

I found Wendy in the library.

"Are you looking for book one of *Devotions for Super Average Kids*?" I asked. "I hear the author is really cute."

"Stay away from me!" Wendy said. "I don't want to get sick."

"Uh, about that. Don't tell Karen, but I don't really have the swine flu, and I lied about not being home yesterday."

"Why'd you lie to Karen?" Wendy asked. "One of the reasons I like you is because you're a Christian. But Christians don't lie, do they?"

It took me a minute to answer, because my mind kept replaying the part where Wendy said she liked me.

"Uh . . . yeah. You're right," I finally said. "Christians let their yes be yes and their no be no. I don't know why I lied. I did it the first time Karen called, and it just got easier and easier. I'm sorry I let you down."

Wendy smiled and said, "Well, I'm sorry you missed Splash City. Maybe we can all go later this summer. By the way, I like your pants today. You should wear plaid more often."

Super Average Advice

Do you have any friends who lie to you all the time? Maybe they do it to spare your feelings. Some kids lie to make themselves look better in a story. Others just lie out of habit.

There are always those kids who spew lies. If you know one, this scene probably sounds familiar:

Josh: I think Jason has been lying to me.

Andy: How can you tell?

Josh: His lips have been moving.

Okay, that's an old joke. But lying goes waaaay back too.

How far? you ask.

Well, "In the beginning God created the heavens and the earth"

(Genesis 1:1). And shortly after that, the serpent said to the first woman, "No! You will not die. . . . God knows that when you eat [the fruit] your eyes will be opened and you will be like God" (Genesis 3:4–5). That's not just one lie. Satan packed several lies in his words to Eve. Because when she and Adam ate the fruit from the Tree of the Knowledge of Good and Evil, they did die (though not right away), and they were also forced out of the garden of Eden. Plus—and this is much more important—we can never become like God. Sure, we can strive to follow Jesus and become more like Him. But we'll never be equal, which is what Satan has always wanted, because only God is totally perfect and holy.

Satan lied to Eve at the beginning of the world, and he continues to try and fill our heads with lies today. Jesus even called Satan the "father of lies" in John 8:44 (ESV).

When we lie, we're not following God's plan for our lives. He wants us to speak the truth, even if it means we'll get in trouble. Also, the truth is, when we lie, we always end up in trouble anyway.

Proverbs 19:5 says, "A false witness will not go unpunished, and one who utters lies will not escape." We often tell lies to try to "escape." We bend the truth with a teacher to get extra time on a homework assignment. We lie to our parents to avoid punishment. But God's Word says that when we utter lies, we'll get caught . . . and sometimes miss out on fun waterslides. (Okay, that last part isn't really in there.)

That's the honest truth!

God's Guide

Read: Leviticus 19:11

1. Why do you think God told Moses to include these words when He gave His people the laws of holiness?

   _____

   _____

   _____

2. How is acting deceptively like lying? Is telling only part of the truth still lying?

   _____

   _____

   _____

BONUS ACTIVITY

Create your own waterpark by taking a bucket of water to a local park. Climb to the top of a slide, pour out the water, and then go sliding after it. If that doesn't work, ask your parents to go to a *real* waterpark.

Someone to Watch Over Me

ongratulations!" Dad said. "I see Wendy's going to church with us tomorrow."

"How'd you know?" I asked. "Was it on Fox News already? She just told me, so how'd she have a chance to do an interview?"

"I read your text," he reminded me.

You see, my parents read my text messages. When I receive a text, it also goes to my parents' phones. This still surprises me, mostly because my dad's not very good with technology. He can't even watch TV unless someone's there to show him how to work the remotes.

Once he sat down to watch a football game, grabbed our three remotes, and started pressing buttons. Instead of turning on the game, he turned on the radio, the DVD player, and the DVR. He sat there watching a cooking show while the sounds from a Toby-Mac song and VeggieTales video competed with each other! It actually made the cooking show better that way.

Anyway, technology is not Dad's friend. But the second I got a cell phone, he somehow figured out how to make my texts go to his phone as well. I told him it was an invasion of privacy! As an American citizen, I had a right to private texting. He laughed at that for about an hour.

Then he explained why our family had that rule.

"I'm your dad, and it's my job to guide you through this world," he said. "That means being involved in everything. I'm here to protect, to lead, and to teach you. Plus, I'm paying all the bills. Now show me how to turn on this TV so I can watch my show."

It's not just texts either. I'm not allowed to lock my bedroom door. My parents look through my backpack. They read my emails. They even have a GPS tracking app on their phones that shows them where I'm at! Actually, it just shows them where my phone is, so one time I played a trick on them.

Billy and his dad had to fly to Michigan for the day. I gave Billy my phone because I knew my dad would check on me. Imagine his surprise to see I was in Detroit!

Okay, only my phone was in Detroit. I was helping my youth leader paint the youth room at church. I got lots of laughs from that. Most of the laughs came from the policeman when Dad had me call and cancel the search. Those Detroit cops are awesome!

Anyway, I have no privacy. At first I was mad. Then I realized that my dad was right. My parents care about me and need to protect me any way they can. Sometimes I still get frustrated. But my mom said that if I have nothing to hide or be ashamed of, then it shouldn't be a big deal. I couldn't argue with that.

But I also couldn't help having a little fun. I called Wendy and set up a plan. Twenty minutes later, my dad burst into my room.

"You're not going anywhere!" he shouted.

You see, I had Wendy send me a fake text that said, "Hey, AB. I'm running away. Go with me! We can jump trains and travel the world and Arkansas!"

Then I texted back, "Sure. Give me 10 minutes!"

Well, Dad didn't give me 10 minutes. He started his lecture, but then his phone buzzed again. He paused and read the next text from Wendy: "Just kidding, Mr. Smiley! AB just wanted to mess with you."

At first I couldn't figure out how he was going to react; then he let out a deep laugh that sounded like a growl.

"You got me," he said, sitting down on my bed. "But that's nothing to joke about."

"I know," I said. "And even though it's sometimes frustrating, I'm glad you and Mom love me enough to watch over me."

He smiled and gave me a nice long hug. At least that's what I thought he was doing. Turns out he had grabbed my phone. Ten

Did You Know?

- More than 90 percent of parents feel their children share too much personal information online, and they want more Internet privacy protection.
- The Global Positioning System (GPS) was developed for the US Department of Defense, costing $12 billion. In 1996, GPS was made available for public use.
- Before GPS, parents tracked their children using bloodhounds and homing pigeons—but that was a lot messier . . . and smellier.

minutes later I found my phone in the kitchen with a confusing text message from Wendy.

My dad had sent her this message: "The trick worked! U r the best! 2 bad I'm such a goofy booger head! CUL8R, Snugglewubbles!"

Some jokes are not funny.

Super Average Advice

As you grow, you may experience the desire for greater privacy. When that time comes, ask yourself, *Why do I want more privacy?* Then ask, *Is this a good reason?* Here are some examples to help:

- You want more privacy so you can read the Bible. Good reason.
- You desire more alone time because you want to search for whatever you want on the Internet. Bad reason.
- Greater privacy would allow you to fully develop your plan for world domination. Bad reason.
- With increased privacy, you could knit more baby caps to give to your local hospital. Good reason.

Okay, maybe that wasn't too helpful. The biggest question to ask yourself when it comes to this issue is, *Do I want more privacy so I can hide things from my parents?*

If that's the case, don't expect too much privacy. Your parents know you best, so if they feel you pulling away, they'll do what it takes to stay in your life and keep track of what you're doing.

Wanting privacy isn't bad. Some things are done best in private. The Bible tells us to pray privately (Matthew 6:6). And just a few verses before that, it says we shouldn't make a big show about helping other people, but instead do it privately (Matthew 6:3). But if you want privacy to experiment with smoking, drinking alcohol, or unhealthy relationships, you should know it won't work.

Proverbs 28:13 says, "The one who conceals his sins will not prosper, but whoever confesses and renounces them will find mercy." That's a pretty clear message. Your sins will be discovered, so there's no reason to be private about them. Instead, it's best to confess them and commit to changing your behavior.

Basically, when it comes to privacy, if you have nothing to hide, then there's no reason to hide it. Live your life as if it's being projected on a 50-foot-tall movie screen for everybody to see. Not much privacy there. And the truth is, that's exactly how you're living.

Hebrews 4:13 tells us, "No creature is hidden from Him, but all things are naked and exposed to the eyes of Him to whom we must give an account." God knows all and sees all. Nothing can be kept private from Him, because He knows our thoughts and actions. Everything we do is exposed to Him—He doesn't even need a GPS tracker. And He loves us anyway!

So if you want more privacy, talk with your parents. Be honest about your reasons. Respect their decision. You may be surprised where the conversation goes, especially if they say, "Don't be such a goofy booger head!"

God's Guide

Read: Ephesians 5:11–14

1. These verses say that actions done in secret can be shameful.
    Why do you think people try to hide the bad things they do?

    _____

    _____

    _____

2. Can you hide anything from God? If you have no privacy
    from God, how much privacy do you think you need from
    your parents?

    _____

    _____

    _____

BONUS ACTIVITY

If your family has a cell phone with GPS, go to a geocaching website and seek out some hidden treasures near your home. If you don't have a GPS, check out websites for letterboxing and use the clues to hunt down secret stashes.

25

Read All About It

"What are you reading for?" Donny asked me.

I didn't know how to answer. If he'd asked what I was reading, I could have answered him. But he asked me, "What are you reading for?"

"I guess I'm reading so my brain will be filled with great knowledge. Then I won't have to spend the next four years repeating the same grade with you," I joked.

The problem with real life is that you can't add "I joked."

Donny didn't understand this was a joke. He grabbed me and dragged me over to a big chair. This was pretty impressive because I was already sitting in a chair.

"I prefer the chair I'm in," I said.

We were in shop class at the time. Our teacher, Mr. Clark, had assigned us a project to make nets out of rope. I'd finished, which is why I was reading.

Donny had dragged me to the chair that was in front of all the ropes. He quickly started tying me up. I looked around for Mr.

Clark. Sure enough, I could see him through the window in his office.

Mr. Clark likes to give an assignment and then go into his office to meditate on the next assignment. He does this by laying his head on the desk and closing his eyes. If he's really into it, he'll even make grumbling noises that sound like snoring.

Donny tied my hands behind my back and said, "Let's see your brain get you out of this."

Well, last month I'd read a survival book that said to remain calm in any situation.

"Not so smart now, huh?" Donny smiled. "Guess you didn't read a book on knots!"

That's when it hit me. I *had* read a book on knots! Billy and I had made a rope swing two years ago by tying a rope to a tree branch. Our idea was to grab the rope, swing over a creek, and splash into the water.

Well, the first attempt proved I didn't know how to tie knots.

Did You Know?

- Kids who read a lot tend to be stronger writers and are better able to concentrate.
- Guinness World Records recognized Howard Berg as the world's fastest reader. He can read 25,000 words a minute. The average person reads about 200 words a minute.
- Your eyes read the same way together. Aren't you glad God made it that way? Otherwise you might end up cross-eyed.

As I swung on the rope, the knot came untied, and instead of landing in the water, I landed on the ground . . . and on one now jittery cat. After that little setback, I went home and found a book on knots.

Sitting in the chair, I reached back and felt the knots. Donny had used a "handcuff" knot. I simply undid it with my fingers. But instead of throwing off the rope, I held the rope in my hand to make it look like I was still tied up.

"If I can get out, will you let me go back to reading my book?" I asked.

"Yeah." Donny grinned. "When you get out, you can grab your book and pick up your diploma from high school. Because that's how long you're going to be there!"

He turned and walked away. I stood up and followed him. He got six steps away and turned around so quickly that I ran into him.

"Sorry, Donny," I said. "My book's this way."

Donny stared at me for a second and then laughed.

"Wow, maybe I should read more. You don't have a book on knots, do you?"

"Not with me," I said.

Anyway, being a reader has saved me in many situations. Most of those times, it's been because of something I've read in the Bible. God's given us the best survival handbook of all time. The more you read it, the more help you'll get.

I'm assuming you're already a reader, because you're reading this book. Just make sure you're reading the right words, and more important, God's Word! Now if you'll excuse me, I have to go wake up Mr. Clark before Donny finds a book on knots.

Super Average Advice

In the early 1800s, Sir William Curtis gave a speech at a board of education dinner in England, where he said that the basic skills every child needed to learn in school were the three Rs—reading, writing, and arithmetic.

Strangely, only one of those words actually begins with *r*.

Although Sir William's spelling might have been a little off, his sentiment was correct. Reading, writing, and arithmetic truly are the building blocks of learning.

In countries where literacy rates are high, people tend to thrive. The United States, Canada, and Japan all have literacy rates around 99 percent for people 15 and older. In other countries, such as Ethiopia and Mali, only four out of every 10 people can read. In those places, it's hard for kids to get an education. And without a good education, people have a hard time improving their lives.

We read for many reasons:

- To learn
- To escape into the world of imagination
- To do research
- To be entertained
- _____ (fill in why you read)

One of the main reasons you read as a Christian is to learn about God. In the Old Testament, God instructed the king to write a list of His instructions. Then the king had to "read from it all the days of his life, so that he may learn to fear the LORD his God, to observe all the words of this instruction, and to do these statutes" (Deuteronomy 17:19).

How often do you read God's instructions in the Bible? Every day? The more you read, the more you'll understand. As the apostle Paul wrote in 2 Corinthians 1:13, "We are writing nothing to you other than what you can read and also understand. I hope you will understand completely."

As you know from school, reading comprehension is important. And it's doubly important when it comes to God's Word. If you don't understand something you read in the Bible, ask a parent or youth leader what it means.

So when it comes to school, remember the three Rs. And when it comes to reading the Bible, remember these three Rs: read regularly, use resources, and memorize all you can. (Hey, at least two of those three Rs are words that start with _r_.)

God's Guide

Read: Romans 15:4 and 2 Timothy 3:16

1. According to these verses, why was the Bible written?

   _____

   _____

   _____

2. What are some good reasons to read the Bible? Try to plan a little Bible reading time every day. Start at one minute and work up from there.

   _____

   _____

   _____

BONUS ACTIVITY

Try saying this 10 times fast without messing up: "You ought not get caught tying naughty knots." Then go check out a knot-tying book from the library . . . just in case you end up in a class with Donny.

26

Some Assembly Required

We had a school assembly today. I love school assemblies because we get out of class. I mean, we get to learn something new.

We've had all kinds of motivational speakers in past assemblies. One guy talked to us about dealing with anger. He asked if anyone struggled with a short temper. I quickly raised a hand.

He pointed out that we weren't supposed to raise *other* people's hands. I had grabbed Donny's hand, knowing that, as the class bully, he had major anger issues. I said that Donny was asleep and couldn't respond properly.

"In fact," I added, trying to prove my point, "look how angry he is now that he's awake."

Another motivational speaker talked to us about staying focused at school and, uh . . . something else. I drifted off after his first story. But I remember he was good. By "good" I mean he talked longer than he was supposed to, and we ended up missing three classes!

My favorite speaker talked to us about different careers we could

choose later in life. He asked us to shout out some talents we have
that might turn into careers.

"I have the talent to shout things out," I shouted, making everyone laugh—and Donny stir in his sleep.

One kid shouted that he didn't have any talents. I suggested he
could always speak at school assemblies for a living. The speaker
didn't seem to appreciate my help.

Today's speaker was going to talk about making good decisions.
As everybody filled the gym, I took my newly assigned seat between
my teacher and the principal.

The speaker came out wearing a bright-red shirt, a yellow tie,
and a blue jacket. He looked like someone hit him with a newly
painted rainbow.

Anyway, I figured he wore that outfit as an example of a bad
decision that could easily be made. Turns out he never talked about
it. It did, however, get me to start thinking about some bad decisions I'd made recently. The first one that came to mind was the day
I decided to wear two different shoes to school. I couldn't find my
sneakers, so I grabbed a boot and a church shoe. This made one foot
heavier than the other, so I walked in big circles all day.

I made another bad decision when I missed the school bus and
decided I could get to school on my skateboard . . . holding on to
the bumper of a car. I realized this was a bad decision the first time
the car hit its brakes and I hit its bumper.

But the decision that really stuck out in my mind was how I'd
acted at the other school assemblies. I knew shouting out funny

things got a laugh, but I also knew it was disrespectful. My principal had told me there were kids at school who really needed to hear some of the speakers' advice.

"Not every kid has a good life like yours, Bob," she said. "So you need to allow them to get the help they need."

She had a point. I knew those speakers had helped kids, and I shouldn't distract from that even if it didn't interest me. I decided I wouldn't shout out things at school assemblies. But just then, the speaker asked for kids to shout out things we were working on in our lives.

Without thinking I yelled, "I'm trying not to shout out things at school assemblies!"

The speaker smiled and said I had a long way to go. My principal disagreed: "You have a short way to go right now," she said. "Off to my office, Bob!"

Sometimes it's fun to be the class clown, but as Christians, we have to know when our actions are funny and when they're disrespectful. The Bible tells us to respect those around us, especially adults. Respect is a lesson I'm still learning, but I'm getting better at it . . . one trip to the principal's office at a time.

Super Average Advice

How would you act in these situations?

1. Your aunt is talking to you about her knitting club. You have no interest in the subject, so you

a. look at your cell phone, hoping that somebody has texted you.

b. start humming the tune to your favorite song.

c. interrupt her, saying, "Did you say club? Let me tell you about my soccer club."

d. suddenly shout, "Bee! Bee!" as you run around madly swinging your arms in the air.

e. listen, ask a question about the club, and then after a while excuse yourself from the conversation.

2. You see an older man with his arms full of stuff walking toward a door at the mall. You

a. run in front of him to get outside more quickly.

b. get out your phone so you can take a video of him smashing into the door and dropping his stuff.

c. zip in front of him so you can open the door.

Did You Know?

- School assembly speakers may charge as little as $500 to as much as tens of thousands of dollars.
- Many people who identified themselves as class clowns in school went on to pursue fields in the manufacturing industry. Seven percent of former class clowns earn more than $100,000 a year.
- The worst title for a school assembly may be "Beets: It's What's Missing from Your Cafeteria."*

*Maybe you can think of a funnier title. Go to *averageboy.org* and send us your best ideas for a silly school assembly. We may even post some of them on the website.

Although all of the answers may be tempting, the proper re-
sponses are *e* and *c*, which also happen to be two letters in the word
R-E-S-P-E-C-T.

The Bible talks a lot about respect. Respect for the elderly. Respect for God. Respect for government officials. Respect for parents.
Respect for . . . well, everybody.

In the two situations, you show respect by listening and helping.
It's disrespectful to blow off a conversation or ignore a person who
needs your help.

Showing respect can be as simple as saying please and thank you
or as difficult as holding your tongue and allowing someone else to
talk when you want to interrupt.

Romans 13:7 says, "Pay your obligations to everyone: taxes to
those you owe taxes, tolls to those you owe tolls, respect to those
you owe respect, and honor to those you owe honor." Notice that it
says you "owe" respect. A lot of kids believe their respect has to be
earned before it can be given. That may be true in some relationships. But when it comes to parents, teachers, police officers, pastors, government officials, and others in authority, the Bible says you
"owe" them your respect. It's your duty to respect them—or at least
the position they hold. However, you can evaluate authority figures
by their actions. If someone in authority asks you to do something
that's against the law or what you know God wouldn't want you to
do, it's still wrong. At that point you need to get away and immediately tell an adult you trust what happened.

As important as it is to show respect for the people in your life, you should always show respect to God. Deuteronomy 8:6 (NIrV) says, "Obey the commands of the LORD your God. Live as he wants you to live. Have respect for him."

God deserves our respect. We demonstrate respect by serving Him and following His commands.

Living with respect isn't hard, but it does take a little extra thought and action.

God's Guide

Read: 1 Peter 2:17

1. According to this verse, whom do you need to show respect?

   _____

   _____

   _____

2. Define what it means to show respect in your own words. Write down specific ways you can show respect for the different people in your life.

   Parents: _____

   Siblings: _____

   Grandparents: _____

   Teachers: _____

   Friends: _____

   Pastor: _____

   Police: _____

Bonus Activity

Wear two different shoes to school and see how long it takes anybody to notice.

27

Pop Up and Get Out

y dad likes to tell me stories from way back in prehistoric days. You know, back when the years started with 19 instead of 20. Today he told me how they didn't have the Internet when he was growing up.

"We didn't have Twitter or Facebook. The status update hadn't even been invented yet! When I fed my cat and wanted people to know, I had to call them individually. By the time I was done with my phone calls, it was time to feed the cat again!"

He was joking, of course.

I had just told him that Wendy texted me that she tweeted about feeding her cat. He thought it was funny that she was texting about tweeting. Technology can consume our lives if we aren't careful. I know this is a fact. I just spent an hour Googling it. The Internet, especially, can be a huge time waster. And last week I found out it can be dangerous.

Monday afternoon I sat down to check my email. I don't think my email works right, because I hardly ever get messages from my friends. This time, however, I had something in my in-box!

A guy in Spain wanted to know if I would accept $2 million in my bank account! He said that he'd done tons of research on me. He said he selected me because I was trustworthy and knew a good deal when I saw it. All I had to do was send him $300 for legal fees, along with my social security number and bank account details. That's it. Then I'd never have to mow a lawn again!

Well, I'm no dummy. I knew there had to be a catch. First, I would have to get a bank account. I guess his research wasn't too good, because I keep all my money in a sock in my closet. I thought about sending him a photo of my sock but didn't know how he'd get the money transferred into it. Then I thought of another glitch. I would most likely have to pay for the stamp to mail him the $300. I emailed him back, asking if he'd pay for the stamp out of the $2 million he was giving me. Told you I was no dummy!

Well, this guy was itching to get rid of his money because he emailed me right back! He asked where I lived. They must have cheap flights from Spain to Texas because he said he could meet me at the nearest mall. I made a mental note to bring my sock. But before emailing him back, I asked my dad where the nearest mall was. Thank goodness I did! That's how I found out about scams and Internet predators.

Dad told me about scams where people use the Internet to trick others into sending them money. It happens all the time. He also told me about how kids are targeted on the Internet as well.

"Bob, never talk to someone online that you don't know," he

said. "I've told you that before. And if they ever ask to meet you somewhere, tell an adult right away. Evil people pretend to be someone else online. They build up trust and then ask to meet. It's very dangerous and can lead to kidnapping."

So I emailed the guy back, saying he could meet me at the nearest police station. I never got a reply. But while I was waiting, I Googled "Internet scams." My dad was right! A ton of websites popped up, talking about scams like the one I just saw.

I clicked on a website about scams. (That's another danger of the Internet.) Any time you click on something, you let the outside world into your house. As I started reading, a pop-up ad appeared on my screen for a new video game called The Warrior Princess.

It sounded cool, so I clicked on it. Well, I don't know where this princess lives, but it must be really warm there! She barely had any clothes on. I try to guard my eyes and heart against stuff like that, so I was trying to close the page when my dad walked in.

"What are you looking at?" he shouted.

Did You Know?

- People lose more than $240 million a year in Internet scams.
- One in four children has accidentally seen violent or inappropriate images on the Web by clicking on a pop-up ad or an unfamiliar website.
- In 1995, only one in 10 adults regularly went online in the United States. By 2011, that number skyrocketed to nearly 80 percent of adults and 95 percent of teenagers.

"I just clicked on an ad, and she popped up," I said, turning red from embarrassment.

I quickly apologized and decided not to click on sites I didn't know anything about. It's too dangerous. My dad and I made some new Internet rules, such as having a parent close by when I'm searching for things, to help me guard my eyes.

I just wish we'd closed out the website before talking about the new rules. My mom walked into the room and screamed, "What are you showing our son?!"

Now it was Dad's face that turned red.

Super Average Advice

The Internet is a place where you can have fun, laugh at silly videos, and even play Average Boy games . . . if you go to *averageboy.org*. But there's nothing funny about online dangers. You need to do everything you can to be wise as you surf the Web. Check out your "Web wisdom" by answering these questions:

1. True or false: Giving out personal information to register for online kids' clubs or contests is a bad idea.

2. True or false: Downloading free cool-looking software could give my computer a virus.

3. True or false: A friend your age from a kids-club website wants to meet you. It's best to tell your parents about this request before responding.

4. True or false: It's okay to give someone online a photo of you.

All the answers are true, except for question four. You should never send a photo of yourself to somebody who's not a friend or family member. Though the answers may seem obvious, the dangers of the Internet are real, and you could lose way more than the money in your sock!

Not only do you need to guard your heart from dangerous websites; you also need to guard information about yourself from evil people who target children online. The police and FBI have experts working around the clock to capture predators who go after children. So if you ever experience something that makes you uncomfortable online, tell a parent right away.

When it comes to using the Internet, you can never be too safe. And the following ideas will help keep you even safer.

The heart of the matter. If you've prayed to ask Jesus to forgive your sins and be Lord of your life, God's Spirit lives inside you. But sometimes your actions don't reflect your faith in Christ. We all make mistakes. Maybe you've made some mistakes with what you've seen on the Internet. If that's the case, pray and ask God to forgive you. Psalm 51:10 (ESV) says, "Create in me a clean heart, O God, and renew a right spirit within me."

God cleans your heart and helps you live for Him. You can rely on Him to help you overcome the temptations found on the Internet.

The eyes have it. What you watch matters. Have you ever heard the saying, "The eyes are the gateway to the soul"? When you see something, it goes to your heart and can burn an image into your brain. Proverbs 23:26 says, "My son, give me your heart, and let your eyes observe my ways." As much as you can control it, your eyes should focus on things that are good, joyous, and encouraging. By following that plan, you'll be better able to stay out of the tangled Web and still enjoy the online world.

God's Guide

Read: Philippians 4:8

1. The Internet can be filled with gossip, rumors, misinformation, inappropriate photos, and bad language. According to this verse, what does God want you thinking about?

    _____

    _____

2. How does your mind feel when you think about nasty things? How do you feel when you think of good things? Which is better?

    _____

    _____

    _____

BONUS QUESTION

Does your family have an Internet filter to block harmful websites? If not, talk to your parents about getting one. The best Internet filter is to look on the back of your computer for a cord. Then unplug it!

Time Is Not on Your Side

Some people think kids are lazy. And by "some people" I mean my dad. I wrote that because he's standing next to me right now.

I told him I was going to write about what happened yesterday. He's reading over my shoulder to make sure I leave out two embarrassing parts. But he's leaning so close I can tell he had egg salad and coffee for breakfast. Okay, now he says I need to leave out three things. I'm sure I'll remember to delete that coffee-and-egg thing before this book gets published.

Anyway, yesterday Dad and I were talking about how technology makes kids lazy. This topic came up because I was eating a motorized lollipop. The motor actually spins the candy!

I was sitting in the kitchen with my tongue pressed against the spinning lollipop when my dad walked in and said, "Are kids too lazy to lick their own candy?"

"Yes," I quickly said. "Now can you hold my tongue out for me! I'm getting tired."

He tried to grab my tongue, and we both had a good laugh. Then he asked if I wanted to invite some friends to play baseball.

I told him I needed to work on this book.

"Bob," he said in a sympathetic voice, "the three people who are going to buy it can wait an extra day."

"Hardy, har, har," I said, turning my lollipop back on.

I love it when Dad plays baseball with my friends and me. He likes to pitch for both teams. This means no one ever strikes out. When he throws the ball, you have plenty of time to think about how you want to hit it and where you want to hit it and finish your chores. You can even read a book (hopefully this one) before you have to swing.

Dad said he'd prefer if his pitching style wasn't included in this chapter. But that's what he gets for going into the kitchen to get some more egg salad and coffee.

Did You Know?

- Spin pops have been around for 20 years, taking away all the difficulty of eating candy. Now the lollipop does all the work!
- Pop Rocks were created in 1956 but weren't sold in stores until 1975. The popping sensation occurs when tiny pockets of carbon dioxide are released as the candy melts in your mouth.
- You've probably waved your hand under a dispenser in the bathroom to get soap. Sharper Image created a motion-sensitive candy machine that gives out something much yummier when you wave your hand.

I began calling my friends to see who could play while Dad got out the baseball stuff. I started with Kyler.

"Can Kyler play baseball?" I asked when his mom picked up the phone.

"Well, he's got basketball practice in thirty minutes," she said. "Then he's got swim class and gymnastics, but chess club was canceled, so I could drop him by after choir practice at around nine thirty."

Whoa! I was tired just listening to all that. I told her I'd take a rain check, which reminded her that Kyler had 4-H tonight. They were making rain catchers.

Then I called Randy. Randy couldn't come because his parents had signed him up to volunteer at an animal shelter. He told me it would look good on his college résumé. I didn't know we had to work with animals in college, but I made a mental note to bring my dog along when I left for college.

I tried three more kids. They all had schedules that prevented them from playing. I even called Colter. Normally I'd never call him because he's too good. It always takes me forever to jump on my bike to retrieve the ball after he hits it. But Colter couldn't come either. His parents had signed him up for football camp. He had to spend two hours a day after school and four hours on Saturdays training so he could get a college scholarship. I told him that if we went to the same college, he could borrow my dog.

As I hung up on my last call, Dad walked back into the house.

"I got the bases laid out and my pitching arm warmed up," he said. "Who's coming over?"

"No one," I said.

"Are they afraid of my fastball?"

"A three-toed sloth isn't afraid of your fastball!" I said.

Then I explained how busy everyone was. My dad frowned.

"Extracurricular activities are good, but you can go overboard," Dad said. "Have you noticed how Randy hasn't been to church on Wednesdays lately? His parents take him to baseball practice instead."

He then said something that gave me a great idea for this chapter.

"How can we as parents want God to be the center of our kids' lives if we're filling their schedules with things that aren't God-centered?"

It was a great point. He made it so emphatically that he didn't realize he'd grabbed an onion instead of an apple from the kitchen counter. Of course, he realized it after his first bite. That's the second thing he didn't want me to mention. But again, that's what he gets for going back for a third cup of coffee!

Super Average Advice

How do you eat a bag of Skittles? Some kids rip open the top, pour a dozen into their mouths, and start chewing. After repeating that technique a few times, their candy is gone before they know it.

Other kids savor their Skittles. They pull a single glossy candy from the package and push it gently past their lips. Then they suck off the shiny shell, enjoying each nuanced flavor. These kids truly "taste the rainbow."

You may be asking, *What does eating candy have to do with*

spending time with family or God? In this case, everything. Because in the example, Skittles aren't Skittles—they're time.

Sometimes it's easy for us to rush through life. We eat through hours without appreciating every minute. We get so busy that life's a blur. Trivial things, such as video games or TV, distract us from God's glorious plans for us.

To get the most out of our time on earth, God wants us to do two things:

1. Be still. We're called human beings, not human doings. But we often end up doing a lot. We find ourselves overwhelmed with school, sports, and extracurricular activities. But too much of a good thing is too much.

Psalm 46:10 (ESV) reminds us to "be still, and know that I am God." That doesn't mean that God wants us to sit around picking the fuzz out of our belly buttons. (Although you may be able to knit a weird blanket by doing this.) God wants us to work, to sharpen the talents and skills He has given us. But by slowing down, we're able to focus on God and appreciate His power. When we're too busy to spend time with God, we're missing out on the ultimate power source.

2. Be wise. Every day God gives us is precious. Planning for the future and working toward college scholarships is a good use of time. But we can't forget about God. Part of being His followers means making Him the center of our lives. The apostle Paul wrote, "Act wisely toward outsiders, making the most of the time" (Colossians 4:5). When we act wisely and show God's love to those around us, He will bless our efforts . . . and our time.

God's Guide

Read: Ephesians 5:15–17

1. According to these verses, how do wise people use their time?

_____

_____

_____

2. As you look at your schedule, what activities honor God the most? Is there anything you could add to your schedule (or take away) to make the most of your time?

_____

_____

_____

• • • • • BONUS ACTIVITY • • • • •

When Pop Rocks first showed up in stores, people thought eating them and drinking soda would make their stomachs explode! The candy maker spent thousands of dollars to take out advertisements proving it wasn't true. It was just a myth. Try it and see what happens. Add a Mentos to the mixture if you want to really feel some poppin'!

Out of the Woods

hy can't we just camp here?" I said, readjusting my backpack. "I'm tired of all this hiking."

"Because we're still in my backyard," Mike answered. "We want to hike into the woods before setting up camp."

Tonight I was camping out with some new friends. I normally hang out with Billy, but he got grounded for making Jell-O. I didn't hear all the details, but I do know Billy's dad was not happy when he went to take a bath.

As I rode the bus home today, I heard Mike and Trent talking about camping out. They were talking loudly so I'd obviously overhear and ask to go. I figured they knew I was an expert camper.

"Fine! I'll go with you," I said.

Trent looked at Mike and said, "You think Bryce would be cool with it?"

"Sure," Mike said, turning to me. "Get to my house at five thirty with camping gear and eight dollars. We'll explain everything at camp."

Eight dollars? Didn't they know there aren't stores in the woods? They had so much to learn.

The teaching began the second we decided on a camping spot. I started by showing them how to set up a tent by securing it between two trees. This took some time because Trent kept saying that one of the trees looked like it might fall over.

After the tree fell on my tent, I showed them how to break apart the rotted parts for firewood. I told Trent and Mike to make a fire while I set up my tent by theirs.

Now it was time to cook. Trent, Mike, and Bryce found some sticks to use to heat up their hot dogs. Seeing another teaching moment, I pulled out a wire hanger. We had fun taking turns trying to undo my hanger. Then we looked for a stick I could use.

After the meal, things started to go badly. Mike kept looking at his watch. Trent counted his money. Bryce pulled out his phone and made a call. He just listened for a few minutes and then hung up.

"The movie starts at eight thirty," he said, grinning.

"Yeah," I said, thinking he was making a joke. "Forest movies are great. They're all in 3-D! Are we seeing *The Scampering Squirrel* tonight? I hear it's really nutty."

No one laughed. Instead, Mike told me how the campout was just a cover plan. They were going to sneak into town and see a movie. I didn't understand the sneaky part until Trent told me it was an R-rated movie called *The Drunken Postman: Mail Model.*

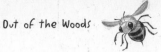

"I'm not supposed to watch R-rated movies," I said. "And that movie is supposed to have a ton of really bad language."

"Come on! You love comedy, and this movie is supposed to be the funniest movie of the year," Bryce said. "Everyone is seeing it."

I knew I had to take a stand. I told them we weren't old enough to buy tickets.

"No problem," Trent said. "We'll buy tickets to another movie and then sneak in. What? Are you afraid?"

"I'm not afraid. I'm just not going," I said. "I told my parents I was camping, so I'm going to camp."

I started trying to bend the wire hanger again.

They kept trying to talk me into going and called me names. Finally they left. I was disappointed, but I wasn't going to let it ruin my campout.

Instead, the strange rustling noises I heard an hour later ruined

Did You Know?

- A whopping $646 billion is spent every year on outdoor recreation. That's more money than people spend on cars!
- Camping was created when Elijah slept in a cave after defeating the prophets of Baal.*
- Tall, dead trees near a campsite are called widow makers for a reason. Never set up a tent anywhere near them.

*You can read the amazing story about Elijah and the prophets of Baal in 1 Kings 18:20–19:9, but camping was around way before this.

it. I left all my stuff behind and ran out of the woods before I could be attacked.

Thirty minutes later, I walked into my house.

"Thought you were camping," Dad said.

"Not a good night for camping," I replied.

"Not a good night to sneak into an R-rated movie either," he said, smiling.

"Uh, what?"

"Your friends got caught sneaking in, and the theater manager called their parents. Mike's mom made Mike call me and explain where you were. Bob, I'm so proud of you for standing up against peer pressure like that!"

Dad walked over and gave me a hug. "Now, where's your brother? I sent him out in the woods to get you."

So that's what that rustling noise was!

Super Average Advice

Peer pressure is the worst. Don't you hate it when you dive way down in the deep end of the pool, start hearing this ringing noise, and get a headache? Or how about when you're in an airplane and get a piercing pain in your head.

Oh wait, that's ear pressure, not peer pressure.

Ear pressure is bad, but it can be avoided by swallowing hard or holding your nose and gently trying to exhale while keeping your mouth closed. Even better, you can just not dive deep underwater or fly.

Peer pressure, on the other hand, is nearly impossible to avoid. At some point your friends will try to get you to do something you know you shouldn't do. Maybe they'll want to try drinking alcohol at a party when parents aren't looking. Perhaps they'll give away all the answers to an upcoming test so everybody can cheat. Or they might try to convince you to watch a movie that your parents wouldn't approve of. Whenever these temptations come, do two things:

1. Stand firm. First Corinthians 16:13 (NKJV) says, "Stand fast in the faith, be brave, be strong." It takes bravery and strength to stand up against peer pressure, because your friends can be very convincing. They'll say things like . . .

- "Don't you want to be my friend?"
- "Everybody else is doing it."
- "It's no big deal."
- "What are you, chicken?"

Your answers should be as simple as "Yes," "Who cares?" "It is a big deal," and "Bawk, bawk." No matter what you say, your actions should speak louder than your words. And your actions should say, "I'm doing what God wants me to do, not what you want me to do."

2. Trust God. Not getting sucked into peer pressure can be hard. Going along with the crowd may seem easier, because nobody wants to feel alone or like a weirdo. When you're tempted to do something that goes against your beliefs, remember this verse: "No temptation has overtaken you except what is common to humanity. God is faithful, and He will not allow you to be tempted beyond what you are able, but with the temptation He will also provide a way of escape so that you are able to bear it" (1 Corinthians 10:13).

Did you get that? Your parents were probably pressured to do the same things you are, because all temptations are "common to humanity." So talk with them about what you're going through with peer pressure. And keep in mind that God will "provide a way of escape."

Sometimes that means walking away. Other times it may mean being alone for a while until you find new friends. But the fact is, you can trust God to help you through any situation.

Of course, you could always just chew gum and yawn. Oh wait, that's ear pressure again.

God's Guide

Read: Galatians 1:10

1. Who do you think is more important to please: God or people? Why?

   _____

   _____

   _____

2. How have you dealt with peer pressure in the past? How can you apply this verse to dealing with peer pressure in the future?

   _____

   _____

   _____

BONUS ACTIVITY

Go camping in your living room and enjoy these benefits:
1. You're never far from food.
2. You can control the temperature and weather.
3. If you ever get scared, you're already home!

Way to Bee!

We went to a bee farm today! On the drive over, my dad said we'd go to a *C* and *D* farm next. We laughed at his joke because he's so clever! Plus, we wanted him to buy us some honey.

Mr. Speck owns the bee farm. He came out to meet us wearing a solid-white jumpsuit and a big white hat with a see-through net hanging over his face.

"Are you getting married today?" I asked.

He just gave me a funny look and explained that beekeepers wear protective clothing to keep the bees from stinging them. I guess that's why a girl wears a veil over her face when she gets married. She doesn't want a nasty bee sting swelling up on her face in her wedding pictures!

Anyway, I thought it'd be cool if a bee stung my upper arms. The whole working-out thing wasn't going too well, so I figured this would make it look like I had huge muscles! Unfortunately, Mr. Speck told all of us to put on white suits.

At first I told Mr. Speck I didn't need a suit because I'd brought a flyswatter that could be transformed into a bee swatter in an emergency. But after taking a look at the field full of thousands of bees, I asked Mr. Speck to make sure my suit was zipped up tight!

We looked like storm troopers on their wedding day. Actually, my dad looked more like a snowman on his wedding day.

Then we headed into a storm of bees. Mr. Speck told us bees make honey from pollen. No other bug does that. Roaches don't make chocolate from leaves. Of course, if they did, I don't think anyone would eat it.

When a bee finds pollen, it goes back to the hive to tell the other bees where the pollen is located. The problem is, bees can't talk very well. They can only say one word—*Bzzzz*. And that's

Did You Know?

- A bee uses a "round dance" if the food source is less than 100 feet away from the hive. In a round dance, the bee circles to the left and the right. If the food is really tasty and plentiful, it dances longer and more energetically.
- A "waggle dance" is used for food far away from the hive. The dancing bee goes in loops and then makes a straight line in the direction of the food. With faster looping and more buzzing, the other bees figure out exactly how far away the food is.
- For a food source located in a tough neighborhood, a bee does the Harlem Shake.*

*Of course this isn't true! The bee actually dances Gangnam Style.

pretty limiting when you're trying to give directions. Bees also can't use electronic devices to tell them where to go. There's no *Bee*PS. So God created bees with amazing dancing ability.

While one bee shakes and dances, the other bees watch. It's sort of like *Dancing with the Stars*—only without all the drama and crying. From watching the one bee dance, the other bees learn where to fly to get the pollen. God is so creative!

By the way, snakes smell with their tongues. This doesn't relate to bees, but I'm just glad humans don't do that. I don't think anyone would wear perfume, because it'd be awkward for a stranger to lick you and say, "Wow, you smell good!"

As we got to the hive, Mr. Speck warned us to be careful because bees fly fast.

"No problem," I said. "I'm super fast too!"

To show him, I decided to run a circle around my brother and dad. About halfway around I got tired and had to stop. Plus, Mr. Speck had already walked off.

By the time we made it to these wooden boxes full of bees, tons of them were flying around my head! They were all shouting the one word they knew, so it was a little hard to hear Mr. Speck, who seemed to be saying something important. I could tell it was important because he was also pointing and nodding his helmet up and down.

I tried doing a little dance to tell the bees to be quiet, but I must have said something else, because they just got louder. My dance also drew more bees to me. I guess they thought I'd found some pollen.

Finally Mr. Speck came over and told me to stand still because I was scaring the bees. Scaring the bees? They have poisonous needles for bottoms that could make me puff up like an inflatable Average Boy, yet I was scaring them? That was funny.

An hour later we were sitting in Mr. Speck's living room eating sweet honey. My dad reminded us that we're all God's worker bees, and we can produce sweetness by showing His love.

It was a great point. But then my brother pretended to be a bee, flew over, and stung me with a plastic sword. Good thing I brought a flyswatter.

Super Average Advice

Have you ever watched the steady hum of activity around a beehive? Scout bees whiz in and out, searching for new sources of food and water. Forager bees buzz to their favorite flowers and fields. Guard bees inspect every bee to keep "robbers" from sneaking in to steal the honey.

In all, thousands of bees work together to benefit the hive. Every bee, regardless of age, has an important duty.

When you think about it, bee families and God's family have a lot in common. Romans 12:4–5 says that followers of Christ are part of a body where each member has a unique and vital function.

Bees stick with the same job until they're old enough to move on to a more complex task. They normally start with cleaning the hive. Then they advance to caring for and feeding baby bees. Next they help build the hive. After handling all of these responsibilities, they earn the privilege of moving outside to guard the hive and search for food.

In God's family, you often find a similar progression. Right now you might be able to help in the church nursery or organize cans in the food pantry. But in the future, you may be called on to lead Bible studies, sing in the church choir, or travel to other countries as a missionary.

Just as the queen is the head of the hive, Jesus is the head of God's body. Ephesians 4:16 says, "From Him [Jesus] the whole body, fitted and knit together by every supporting ligament, promotes the growth of the body for building up itself in love by the proper working of each individual part." From that verse it's obvious that each individual part needs to work properly for the body to function at a top-notch level.

Are you doing your part? List some ways that you are serving and can serve in God's body:

1. _____

2. _____

3. _____

4. _____

5. _____

Another cool thing about bees is that if they notice a job isn't getting done in the hive, they take it on. The bees' willingness to do extra work helps a weak colony become strong and healthy again.

When we look for ways to serve in Christ's body, it produces sweet results. Just think of all you can *bee* for Jesus!

God's Guide

Read: 1 Corinthians 12:14–20

1. Have you ever felt that you didn't have an important job in God's family? What do these verses say about that?

   _____

   _____

   _____

2. Why is it important for bees to have different jobs in the hive? Why is it even more important that we have different roles in God's family?

   _____

   _____

   _____

BONUS ACTIVITY

Honey has numerous health benefits when you eat it, but it's also great for your skin and hair. Next time you wash your hair, squeeze a little honey into your hand and mix it with your conditioner. Rub the mixture into your hair, let it sit for a minute, and then rinse it out. Your hair will shine like never before. You may want to rinse again if you don't want bees following you around all day.

Appendix

Average Boy Online

Visit Average Boy online at *averageboy.org*. You can play games, read more stories, solve puzzles, email Average Boy, and look at some of his past helpful emails.

Here are some samples:

Hey, AB!
Do you like having freckles?
Christopher

Hey, Christopher,
Hmmm, I don't know. I've never *not* had freckles, so there's nothing to compare it to. You might as well ask if I like having ears (which I do like having . . . except when my dad starts snoring).

Freckles can be cool. I once dressed up as a connect-the-dots puzzle for a costume party. And at bedtime I can count freckles instead of sheep, which is way easier because freckles don't wander off midcount.

Most of all, I like my freckles because they're part of how God made me. I may not have movie-star good looks (yet), but I am a one-of-a-kind design.

Your friend and mine,

Average Boy

● ● ● ● ●

What would you do with one million dollars?

Iron Man

Hey, Iron Man,

Congratulations on your movie success! If I had a million dollars, I would be very responsible with it. First, I would give 10 percent to the church. Then I would buy a *few* things. Then I would put the remaining $1,000 in the bank. Oh, and I'd probably legally change my name to Iron Man, because that sounds awesome!

Your friend and mine,

Average Boy

PS: If you ever need a super average sidekick, I might know a guy who can help you . . . if he's not grounded that week.

● ● ● ● ●

Dear Average Boy,

My sister always gets to do stuff that I don't get to do. Sometimes I feel left out. Do you ever feel that way?

Anna

Hey, Anna,

I do now. I didn't know your sister got to do stuff that we didn't. Is it because she's older?

I get to do stuff that my younger brother doesn't, but that's just because I'm older. He'll get to do that stuff when he's my age . . . and he'll probably do it better after watching me make so many mistakes. (He *definitely* won't substitute sour cream on his sandwich when he's out of mayonnaise. I still can't get that nasty taste out of my mouth. *Ugh!*)

Here's something that may make you feel better: If your sister is older, she probably has more chores and responsibilities. So enjoy the age you are and know that life is a fun journey. You don't want to take all the trips at once!

Your friend and mine,

Average Boy

• • • • •

Dear Average Boy,

What's your favorite Bible verse or passage? I've been reading Hebrews, and God has been teaching me a lot. Keep on keeping on!

Hannah

Hey, Hannah,

I'm guessing *your* favorite verse is 1 Samuel 1:5 (esv)—"To Hannah he [her husband] gave a double portion, because he loved her." Your name is in the Bible . . . and for a good reason! (I always feel bad when I meet guys named Shaphat.)

My favorite verse right now—it changes weekly—is John 3:30. Jesus started baptizing everyone. So everyone started going to Him instead of John the Baptist. Well, John's disciples got mad that they weren't the popular group anymore. But John the Baptist made a great speech about Jesus being more important than anyone else. He explained, "He [Jesus] must become more important. I must become less important" (NIrv).

Every day I try to make Jesus greater and myself smaller. Keep reading!

Your friend and mine,

Average Boy

• • • • •

When you grow up, will you be called Average Man?

A Fan in Australia

Hey, Australia Fan,

I love Australia. Y'can probably tell because I'm typing this answer in an Australian accent, mate. And yes, I hope to be called Average Man when I grow up . . . and then move on to Average Old Man. Average Grandpa has a nice ring to it as well! I better start working on growing that beard right away.

G'day, mate, and keep reading!

Your friend and mine,

Average Boy (soon to be Average Man)

• • • • •

Dear Average Boy,

I know that you are supposed to be average, but the mishaps you get into don't seem average to me. Why does something weird always happen to you when you're supposed to be an average boy?

Sincerely,

Heather H.

Hey, Heather!

Good question. Maybe I'm average and everyone else is below average! Hold on, I'll ask . . . Okay, I just asked my dad, but he only rolled his eyes. He does that a lot. You'd think his eyes would be huge now from all the exercise they get. Anyway, I think a lot of stuff happens to me because I'm always doing stuff. I don't just sit around watching TV. I go outside and do stuff like swim or try to get out of the bag Donny put me in. I do a lot of stuff, so a lot of stuff happens to me!

Your friend and mine,

Average Boy

Data Bank of Facts

Chapter 1

The US Centers for Disease Control and Prevention conducted a survey asking kids about avoiding school because of bullying. The results appear in the "Youth Risk Behavior Surveillance System: 2011 National Overview," "Behaviors That Contribute to Violence," http://www.cdc.gov/healthyyouth/yrbs/pdf/us _overview_yrbs.pdf. Bullying statistics also appear in the Youth Risk Behavior Surveillance System publication "Trends in the Prevalence of Behaviors That Contribute to Violence on School Property National YRBS: 1991–2011," US Centers for Disease Control and Prevention, http://www.cdc.gov/healthyyouth/yrbs /pdf/us_violenceschool_trend_yrbs.pdf.

Information on the number of kids bullied in school in 2011 appeared in a report by the US Department of Education: "Student Reports of Bullying and Cyber-bullying: Results from the 2011 School Crime Supplement to the National Crime Victimization Survey," August 2013, no. NCES 2013-329, table 1.1, http://nces.ed.gov/pubs2013/2013329.pdf.

Chapter 2

The Peel P50 is manufactured by Peel Engineering. For photos and information about this cool mini-ride, see "History," http:// www.peelengineering.co.uk/about-us/company/history; and

"Peel P50 Specification," http://www.peelengineering.co.uk
/peels/peel-p50/peel-p50-specification.

No, I don't think your parents will agree to move to Alberta,
Canada, so you can start driving at age 14! But you can learn
more about driving in Canada by visiting ServiceAlberta.gov,
"Drivers/Vehicles: Common questions—Drivers and Motor
Vehicles," http://www.servicealberta.gov.ab.ca/672.cfm; and
"Driver's Licence," http://www.servicealberta.gov.ab.ca/Drivers
_Licence.cfm#Licence_Classes. Check out the driving ages in
other countries at Wikipedia, "List of Countries by Minimum
Driving Age," http://en.wikipedia.org/wiki/List_of_countries
_by_minimum_driving_age.

Wouldn't it be fun to see the Peel P50 and a Bugatti in a drag race? For
more on the Bugatti, see "Most Expensive Cars in the World: Top
10 List 2013–2014," Thesupercars.org, http://www.thesupercars.
org/top-cars/most-expensive-cars-in-the-world-top-10-list/.

Chapter 3

Next time you play Monopoly with your family, why not suggest
the Japanese version? For more information about the game,
see "Monopoly History and Fun Facts," Hasbro.com, "About
Monopoly," http://www.hasbro.com/monopoly/en_US
/discover/about.cfm.

These and other benefits of playing board games can be found at
"The Benefits of Board Games," Scholastic.com,http://
www.scholastic.com/parents/resources/article/creativity-play
/benefits-board-games.

Chapter 4

I couldn't believe that researchers actually study topics like
swearing and then write books about it. One of the experts on
swearing . . . er, *studying* swearing, is Timothy Jay. He published
two brainy scientific articles on the topic: "The Science of
Swearing," *Observer* 25, no. 5, May/June 2012, http://www
.psychologicalscience.org/index.php/publications/observer/2012
/may-june-12/the-science-of-swearing.html; and "The Utility
and Ubiquity of Taboo Words," *Perspectives on Psychological
Science* 4, no. 2 (2009): 155–56, http://people.uncw.edu/hakanr
/documents/useoftaboowords.pdf. Another reader-friendly
article is Hugo Gye and David Gardner, " 'Most Children Learn
How to Swear Before They Even Know the Alphabet': Forget the
ABC, Toddlers Prefer the F Word," *Mail Online*, April 11, 2013,
http://www.dailymail.co.uk/news/article-2307524/Most
-children-learn-swear-know-alphabet-Forget-ABC-toddlers
-prefer-F-word.html.

Chapter 5

With an outdoor TV, kids won't have to miss their favorite shows
when their moms send them outside to get some exercise! See C
Seed Entertainment Systems, "C Seed 201 Giant Outdoor LED
TV" product brochure, "Ingeniously Engineered," http://www
.cseed.tv/fileadmin/user_upload/epaper/#/0. Also see "The TV
So Big You Have to Keep It Outside," *Daily Mail*, January 16,
2013, http://www.dailymail.co.uk/sciencetech/article-2263423

/Porsche-unveils-worlds-largest-TV-boasts-201inch-screen-costs
-414k.html.

I think Richie Woodward's bedroom is about the size of a 1950s
home! This information on house sizes originally appeared in
an article by the National Association of Home Builders titled
"Housing Facts, Figures, and Trends for March 2006." Margot
Adler included a handy chart in her article "Behind the Ever-
Expanding American Dream House," July 4, 2006, NPR.org,
http://www.npr.org/templates/story/story.php?storyId
=5525283.

Estimates of consumer debt vary from year to year, and experts
can never seem to agree on an average amount. I think they
can probably agree that whatever it is, it's not good! Fred O.
Williams talks about this in his article "Average Credit Card
Debt? Take Your Pick," July 8, 2013, CreditCards.com, http://
www.creditcards.com/credit-card-news/average-credit_card
_debt-1276.php.

In a forearm-to-palm snatch Dean Gould caught 328 coins. See
more at "Dean Gould: Records," Record Holders Republic,
http://www.recordholdersrepublic.co.uk/recordholdersdetails
.asp?id=172.

Chapter 6

I wonder how many of those 60 texts were sent to friends who
were at the movies and couldn't text back?! According to Pew
Research, texters between 18 and 24 years of age "send or

receive an average of 109.5 text messages a day," or 3,200 text messages per month! (See Aaron Smith, "Americans and Text Messaging," Pew Internet and American Life Project, September 19, 2011, http://www.pewinternet.org/2011/09/19/americans -and-text-messaging/). Pew Research conducted the texting study in 2011 in their Teens and Digital Citizenship Survey. See the full report in Amanda Lenhart, "Teens, Smartphones, and Texting," Pew Internet and American Life Project, March 19, 2012, http://www.pewinternet.org/Reports/2012/Teens-and-smartphones.aspx.

Read about Austin Wierschke and his lightning-fast texting in the following article: Associated Press, in "Wisconsin Teen Is Fastest Texter in America, *USA Today*, August 8, 2012, http:// usatoday30.usatoday.com/tech/news/story/2012-08-08 /texting-championship/56867966/1.

In 2011, Americans sent more than two trillion text messages, which works out to six billion per day! See Michael O'Grady, "SMS Usage Remains Strong in the US: 6 Billion SMS Messages Are Sent Each Day," *Forrester Blogs*, Forrester Research, June 19, 1012, http://blogs.forrester.com/michael_ogrady /12-06-19-sms_usage_remains_strong_in_the_us_6_billion _sms_messages_are_sent_each_day.

A 2006 survey on cyberbullying not only showed that teens thought cyberbullying was funny, but also six in 10 teens also thought it wasn't a big deal. Read more about cyberbullying in National Crime Prevention Council, "Stop Cyberbullying Before It Starts," http://www.ncpc.org/resources/files/pdf/bullying

/cyberbullying.pdf. If you're interested in the official survey
results, see National Crime Prevention Council, "Teens and
Cyberbullying," February 28, 2007, http://www.ncpc.org
/resources/files/pdf/bullying/Teens%20and%20Cyberbullying
%20Research%20Study.pdf.

Chapter 7

Playing video games 13 hours a day also means that by the time
   kids are 21, they've spent approximately 10,000 hours gaming!
   The original study was published in Douglas A. Gentile,
   "Pathological Video Game Use Among Youth 8 to 18: A
   National Study," *Psychological Science* 20, no. 5 (May 2009):
   594–602, http://drdouglas.org/g2009.html. Another good
   article on gaming is Shannon Younger, "Kids and Video Games:
   What Games Are Safe, and How Much Should They Play?"
   Tween Us (blog), February 27, 2013, http://www.chicagonow
   .com/tween-us/2013/02/kids-video-games-safe-benefits-length
   -time-play/.
In addition to Wiiitis and Nintendo thumb, video gamers can also
   suffer from Burning Bladder and Puzzle Game Hallucinations.
   Read more about gaming injuries at Jennifer L. DeLeo, "A
   Guide to Gaming Injuries," PCMag.com, May 16, 2008,
   http://www.pcmag.com/article2/0,2817,2305624,00.asp.
Limiting screen time to less than two hours a day might seem
   like torture, but it's really a good thing. Trust me! See other
   recommendations in Tia Ghose, "Pediatricians: No More Than
   2 Hours Screen-Time Daily for Kids," *Scientific American*,

October 28, 2013, http://www.scientificamerican.com/article
.cfm?id=pediatricians-no-more-than-2-hour-screen-time-kids.
The original recommendations from the American Academy
of Pediatrics were published in "Policy Statement: Children,
Adolescents, and the Media," *Pediatrics* 132, no. 5 (November
2013): 958–61, http://pediatrics.aappublications.org/content
/132/5/958.full.

Too much time "talking" to friends through tech devices can not
only make you feel disconnected and lonely but can make
you feel uncomfortable with having normal face-to-face
conversations. Sherry Turkle wrote a thought-provoking article
on this topic called "The Flight from Conversation" (*New York
Times*, April 12, 2012). Check it out at http://www.nytimes
.com/2012/04/22/opinion/sunday/the-flight-from-conversation
.html?pagewanted=all&_r=1&.

Chapter 8

The game of miniature golf was created in the 1800s in Europe, but
the word *mulligan* didn't appear until the 1920s or 1930s. It
seems that some guy named Mulligan didn't like a golf shot he
took, so he gave himself a do-over. After that, everyone started
calling replays *mulligans*. No one knows whether this story is
true. Maybe Mulligan hit his brother in the chest with a golf
ball and wanted a do-over. Read about the mulligan and other
golf words in "Golf History FAQ," USGA Museum, http://
usgamuseum.com/researchers/faq/#q9. For other interesting
facts about miniature golf, see Jonathan Haeber, "History of

Miniature Golf," Terrastories.com, http://www.terrastories.com
/bearings/miniature-golf.

Chapter 9

Can you drink too much water? It's possible but hard to do. You'd
have to drink gallons of water—or sweat like a whale!—to cause
dangerously low levels of sodium or *hyponatremia*. For more on
hydration and exercise, see Gina Shaw, "Water Tips for Efficient
Exercise," WebMD.com, "Fitness and Exercise," July 7, 2009,
http://www.webmd.com/fitness-exercise/features/water-for
-exercise-fitness.

For more information about the LoToJa Classic, see "About
LoToJa," LoToJaClassic.com, http://www.lotojaclassic.com
/main/index.html.

Pedersen's original bike design included a wood frame, a fixed gear,
and "cow horn" handlebars as a footrest. Later Pedersen designed
and produced tandem bicycles as well as triplets, quads, and
folding bicycles. Read the full story at "History," Pedersen
Bicycles, http://www.pedersenbicycles.com/history.htm.

Chapter 10

The student homework survey came from the 2008 National
Survey of Student Engagement (NSSE), *Promoting Engagement
for All Students: The Imperative to Look Within—2008 Results*
(Bloomington, IN: Indiana University Center for Postsecondary
Research, 2008), 11, http://nsse.iub.edu/NSSE_2008_Results
/docs/withhold/NSSE2008_Results_revised_11-14-2008.pdf.

On a more positive note, almost half of first-year students
volunteered in community service.

This planet is literally crawling with insects! On top of 900,000
species, scientists estimate that 10 quintillion insects (that's a
ten with 18 zeroes) are alive at this moment in time. Think
about it! In just one ant nest in Jamaica, scientist discovered
630,000 ants. I'd like to know how they counted them all! For
more creepy-crawly insect facts, see Department of Systematic
Biology, "Number of Insects (Species and Individuals)," National
Museum of Natural History, "Bug Info," sheet no. 18, http://
www.si.edu/Encyclopedia_SI/nmnh/buginfo/bugnos.htm.

Chapter 11

For more stinky-animal facts, check out "The Smelliest Creatures on
Earth," Environmental Graffiti, http://www.environmental
graffiti.com/news-smelliest-creatures-alive.

Mum deodorant wasn't actually made from mums. It contained zinc
oxide, the same stuff that's used as a natural sunscreen. Modern
deodorants are sold in many different forms. Aerosol deodorants
are popular in Europe, while stick or solid deodorants are
popular in the US. A book has even been written about the
history of antiperspirants and deodorants, appropriately titled
Antiperspirants and Deodorants (edited by Karl Laden, 2nd ed.,
New York: Marcel Dekker, 1999; see pages 1–3, 276). See
also Mary Bellis, "The History of Commercial Deodorants,"
About.com, http://inventors.about.com/od/dstartinventions/a
/deodorants.htm.

Chapter 12

House sitters usually charge extra for taking care of pets, especially cats that go *sccccaaaahhhhh*. For more information, see Nancy Parode, "Should You Hire a House Sitter?" About.com, http://seniortravel.about.com/od/travelsafety/a/HouseSitter.htm.

Funny that the pet survey didn't include the number of people who own cats that go *scccaaaahhhh*. It did show that 55 percent of cat owners have more than one cat, while 70 percent of dog owners are content with just one dog. The cat-dog data came from the 2013–2014 American Pet Products Association Pet Owners Survey, published in Humane Society of the United States, "US Pet Ownership and Shelter Population Estimates," September 27, 2013, http://www.humanesociety.org/issues/pet_overpopulation/facts/pet_ownership_statistics.html.

Accidents from ladders pale in comparison to accidents from clothes, according to the National Electronic Injury Surveillance System (NEISS) data. The number of emergency-room visits from clothing accidents topped 300,000 in 2012. Makes you wonder, doesn't it? See "NEISS Data Highlights: Calendar Year 2012," US Consumer Product Safety Commission, http://www.cpsc.gov/Global/Neiss_prod/2012NeissDataHighlights.pdf.

Chapter 13

Mentors also need to know how to listen well and develop trust and respect to better help their mentees. A mentor can make a big difference in your life. For more information on mentoring, see American Psychological Association, "Tips for Mentors," http://

www.apa.org/pi/disability/resources/mentoring/tips-mentors
.aspx. Also see American Speech-Language-Hearing Association,
"The Benefits of Mentoring," http://www.asha.org/students
/gatheringplace/MentBen/.

Chapter 14

In the 2009 American Freshman Survey, students rated themselves
above average in leadership and drive, intellectual and writing
ability, self-confidence, and public-speaking ability compared with
students from earlier generations. I wonder if they were above
average in humility too. For more information on student self-
confidence, see William Kremer, "Does Confidence Really Breed
Success?" BBC News, January 3, 2013, http://www.bbc.co.uk
/news/magazine-20756247. The survey was discussed in Jean M.
Twenge, W. Keith Campbell, and Brittany Gentile, "Generational
Increases in Agentic Self-Evaluations Among American College
Students, 1966–2009," *Self and Identity* 11, no. 4 (2011):
409–27.

Researcher Roy Baumeister not only concluded that self-control
is more powerful in success than self-esteem or confidence
(see Kremer, "Does Confidence Really Breed Success?" BBC
News, http://www.bbc.co.uk/news/magazine-20756247), but
his review of self-esteem studies showed that success improves
self-esteem, not the other way around. In fact, high self-esteem
didn't actually improve performance or lead to success. The
results were published in Roy F. Baumeister et al., "Does High
Self-Esteem Cause Better Performance, Interpersonal Success,

Happiness, or Healthier Lifestyles?" *Psychological Science and the Public Interest* 4, no. 1 (May 2003): 1–44, http://www.carlson school.umn.edu/Assets/71496.pdf.

Chapter 15

To learn more about Alex and her lemonade stand, see Alex's Lemonade Stand Foundation, "Frequently Asked Questions," http://www.alexslemonade.org/about/faq.

Helping others is also a great way to meet new people and make friends. See Joanna Saison, Melinda Smith, and Gina Kemp, "Volunteering and Its Surprising Benefits," HelpGuide.org, www.helpguide.org/life/volunteer_opportunities_benefits_volunteering.htm. September 2013. The study on happiness and volunteering appears in Francesca Borgonovi, "Doing Well by Doing Good: The Relationship Between Formal Volunteering and Self-Reported Health and Happiness," *Social Science and Medicine* 66, no. 11 (June 2008): 2321–34, http://www.sciencedirect.com/science/article/pii/S0277953608000373.

Cee Cee called her elephant project Elephants Remember Joplin. Read the whole story in Debby Woodin, "Nine-Year-Old Kentucky Girl Knits Elephants for Joplin's Recovery," *Joplin Globe*, August 16, 2012, http://www.joplinglobe.com/topstories/x1685965706/Nine-year-old-Kentucky-girl-knits-elephants-for-Joplins-recovery.

Read more about Zach Hunter and Loose Change to Loosen Chains (LC2LC) at http://www.zachhunter.me/#/loosechange2loosenchains/history.

Chapter 16

Take it from me, body parts definitely don't like being awakened
from a nice nap. All that burning and tingling is just their way
of getting revenge! "What Makes Your Arms, Legs, and Feet
Fall Asleep?" Discovery Fit and Health, "Human Body,"
http://health.howstuffworks.com/human-body/parts/question
552.htm_ga=1.35170082.2087135585.1393440314.

That game of Duck, Duck, Goose also lasted more than 15 minutes.
See Guinness World Records, "Largest Game of Duck, Duck,
Goose," http://www.guinnessworldrecords.com/records-3000
/largest-game-of-duck-duck-goose/.

Read more about photophobia in Richard C. Senelick, "Why Some
People Wear Sunglasses Indoors," *The Blog, Huffington Post*,
June 18, 2012, http://www.huffingtonpost.com/richard
-c-senelick-md/photophobia_b_1598668.html.

The Tapeworm Diet is one of the most disgusting diets I've ever
heard of. Another really weird diet is the Breatharian diet,
introduced in the 1980s, where people breathe air in place
of eating food and drinking water. That diet starved itself to
death, I think. This information came from William Grimes,
ed., *Eating Your Words* (New York: Oxford University Press,
2004), 250–51. Read about other strange diet fads at Denise
Winterman, "History's Weirdest Fad Diets," BBC News, January
1, 2013, http://www.bbc.co.uk/news/magazine-20695743.
Check out weird fashion fads at the Bad Fads Museum,
http://www.badfads.com/fashion/.

Chapter 17

Did you know that the game of soccer is called *football* everywhere
except the United States? So when you visit the FIFA site, you'll
see headlines like "Women's Football Championship Teams
Gearing Up Next Week," but the women won't be wearing pads
and helmets. The only pieces of special equipment for soccer
are cleats and shin guards, unless you count the extra-long socks
or the wild look in a striker's eye just before he or she shoots a
goal. Look for more information about how many people play
worldwide or international soccer events at the FIFA website:
http://www.fifa.com/newscentre/index.html.

For those of you who enjoy math, you'll find stats about goals per
game and other odd facts about soccer goals in Christopher
Anderson and David Sally's book, *The Numbers Game: Why
Everything You Know About Soccer Is Wrong* (New York:
Penguin, 2013), 44–45.

Sometimes even strong players score own goals. Case in point:
Ireland's Richard Dunne, who holds the European Premier
League's record for own goals. Five minutes after being named
"man of the match" in a 2011 contest, he scored an own goal,
which gave away his team's lead. That game was covered by
journalist Henry Winter in "Queens Park Rangers 1 Aston Villa
1: Match Report," *The Telegraph (UK)*, September 25, 2011,
http://www.telegraph.co.uk/sport/football/competitions
/premier-league/8784624/Queens-Park-Rangers-1-Aston-Villa
-1-match-report.html.

The second best soccer ball juggler lasted less than twenty hours. That statistic, as well as Nikolai Kutsenko's world record, is documented in *Soccer Stories: Anecdotes, Oddities, Lore, and Amazing Feats* by Donn Risolo (Lincoln, NE: Bison Books, 2010), 262.

Chapter 18

If you want to avoid spankings, don't move to Texas. That's the state with the highest percentage of kids whose parents have used physical punishment. See Elizabeth T. Gershoff, *Report on Physical Punishment in the United States: What Research Tells Us About Its Effect on Children* (Columbus, OH: Center for Effective Discipline, 2008), http://www.scribd.com/doc/155733334/Report-on-Physical-Punishment-in-the-United-States-What-Research-Tells-Us-About-Its-Effects-on-Children. For the statistic about fifth-graders, see E. T. Gershoff and S. H. Bitensky, "The case against corporal punishment of children: Converging evidence from social science research and international human rights law and implications for U.S. public policy," *Psychology, Public Policy, and Law*, 13, 231–72.

The mom also posted a picture of her boys crying over losing their toys. The photo will prove it's not Average Boy and his brother. To see the evidence, visit Athima Chansanchai, "Mom Sells Kids' Toys on eBay as Punishment," *Today Moms*, February 18, 2011, http://www.today.com/moms/mom-sells-kids-toys-ebay-punishment-124923.

An unruly boy student could also be sent to the girls' cloakroom
(aka bathroom). For a detailed list, see "Pioneer Sholes School:
Discipline of the School," http://www.pioneersholesschool.org
/pages/discipline.html.

Chapter 19

Most of the kids interviewed had no realistic idea how much
money they would make as an adult. Do you know how much
money the average firefighter makes? Find out that, and more,
in David M. Ewalt's article, "When I Grow Up: Kids' Dream
Jobs," Forbes.com, February 26, 2009, http://www.forbes
.com/2009/02/26/starting-second-career-leadership-careers
_dream_jobs.html.

The founder of Mother's Day, Anna Jarvis, disliked the way the
holiday became centered around buying presents for moms. She
spent the rest of her life trying to cancel the holiday! Read more
about Mother's Day at History.com, http://www.history.com
/topics/mothers-day.

Other top jobs include software developer and physical therapist.
Read more at "The 100 Best Jobs," *U.S. News & World Report,*
"Money: Careers," http://money.usnews.com/careers/best-jobs
/rankings/the-100-best-jobs.

Phil Vischer believes kids should be protected from bad influences
on TV. He sets parental controls on the televisions in his home.
The information about living your life for God is from a 2002
interview Mr. Vischer did with Jesse Florea, one of the writers of

this book. The television info can be found at another interview
Mr. Vischer had with journalist Adam Holz at Focus on the
Family's *Plugged In*, "A Candid Conversation with Phil Vischer,"
December 2009, http://www.pluggedin.com/familyroom
/articles/2008/acandidconversationwithphilvischer.aspx.

Chapter 20

Before the industrial revolution, common people had only two sets
of clothing, one for work and the other for public appearances.
For all the info, see the website Truth According to Scripture,
"The Origin of Dressing Up for Church," http://www.truth
accordingtoscripture.com/documents/church-practice/dressing
-up/dressing-up-for-church.php#.Ue_6vHF394s.
Did you know that ripped jeans can cost as much as five hundred
dollars a pair? See Denimblog, August 5, 2008, http://www
.denimblog.com/2008/08/top-10-most-expensive-jeans/.

Chapter 21

In a survey conducted by White Pages, it turns out that more
people find out information about their neighbors through the
White Pages than face-to-face. Perhaps 76 percent of the people
who live near you don't know your name because you haven't
introduced yourself. Be sure to greet your neighbors and help
them out so you get to know them. For the official info, visit
Wired Market, "New Survey: Majority of Americans Know
Their Neighbors' Pets More Than Their Neighbors' Kids," July 13,
2011, http://www.marketwired.com/press-release/new-survey

-majority-americans-know-their-neighbors-pets-more-than-their
-neighbors-kids-1537459.htm.

If you want to be part of the 40 percent who share their faith,
praying for unsaved people is a great way to start. Find out more
about the way Christians share—or don't share—the gospel at
Lifeway Research survey conducted October 14–22, 2011, in
Jon D. Wilke, "Churchgoers Believe in Sharing Faith, Most
Never Do," LifeWay.com, August 13, 2012, http://www.lifeway
.com/Article/research-survey-sharing-christ-2012.

Chapter 22

A Science Buddy from the US Air Force Space and Missile
Operations says a basketball will explode at around 80 psi.
(PSI = pounds per square inch.) Ask your own question at
Science Buddies (ScienceBuddies.org). To see the answer to
this question go to Science Buddies: "Ask an Expert," "How to
measure how much Air Pressure is in a basketball," February 07,
2013, http://www.sciencebuddies.org/science-fair-projects
/phpbb3/viewtopic.php?f=37&t=11482.

You can find more about sports and how to have a good team
experience at "Getting Cut from a Sports Team," Mom's Team,
http://www.momsteam.com/health-safety/emotional-injuries
/cut-from-sports-team/re-examine-cuts-below-high-school
-varsity?page=0%2C2 by Brooke de Lench. But Ms. de Lench
didn't cite where she got her research, so we can't be sure of
her data. (Average Boy is sure her teachers would have given
her an incomplete.) We did some searching, and we think

the exercise information is from the February 15, 2012, issue of the *Journal of the American Medical Association* (JAMA) in the article, "Moderate to Vigorous Physical Activity and Sedentary Time and Cardiometabolic Risk Factors in Children and Adolescents." (We don't know 100 percent because we can't understand all the medical jargon.) Find out more about Michael Jeffrey Jordan's life as a kid growing up in North Carolina. See IMDb.com, "Michael Jordan," http://www.imdb.com/name/nm0003044/bio?ref _=nm_ov_bio_sm.

Chapter 23

If you got to ride on Divertical, you would travel at speeds of more than 65 miles per hour, according to Briana Fasone, "World's Craziest Water Slides," CNN Travel, August 23, 2012, http:// www.cnn.com/2012/08/23/travel/craziest-water-slides-world. You can also find a large surf pool with 9-foot waves at Mt. Olympus Water and Theme park in the Wisconsin Dells. Find out more about all the parks at the Dells at: http://www .wisdells.com/wisconsin-dells-experience/article.cfm?article id=68&sidebar=family-vacation. Is your family going to Orlando anytime soon? Wet 'n Wild boasts a giant sandcastle for little kids! See Florida Water Parks, "Wet 'n Wild Water Park," http://www.floridawaterparks.com /resources/Wet-N-Wild.html. For the age of Wet 'n Wild, go to University of Central Florida Libraries, "Guide to the Wet 'n

Wild Collection, 1975–2002," http://library.ucf.edu/Special
Collections/FindingAids/WetNWild.xml.

Chapter 24

Even teens think their friends share TMI online. See CNN Wire
Staff, October 8, 2010, "Parents Survey Says Social Networks
Don't Protect Kids' Privacy," http://www.cnn.com/2010
/TECH/social.media/10/08/parents.poll/.

Did you know that Mount Everest is getting taller? Scientists know
that because of GPS technology. The Library of Congress has
the history of GPS at the Everyday Mysteries site. Read more at
http://www.loc.gov/rr/scitech/mysteries/global.html.

Chapter 25

Yeah, Average Boy readers! You're smarter than kids who don't read.
To stay ahead, buy more Average Boy books, but also think
about learning to read the newspaper—even online. Researchers
Alice Sullivan and Matt Brown say that type of reading will
keep you smart through high school. See "Reading for Pleasure
Puts Children Ahead in the Classroom, Study Finds," Center
for Longitudinal Studies, September 11, 2013, http://www.cls
.ioe.ac.uk/news.aspx?itemid=2740&itemTitle=Reading+for+ple
asure+puts+children+ahead+in+the+classroom%2C+study+finds
&sitesectionid=27.

The safest place in Howard Berg's childhood environment was the
library. There he developed a love for reading. The whole story

is at World Breaking Records, "Howard Berg—World's Fastest Reader,." http://www.worldbreakingrecord.com/2011/05 /howard-berg-worlds-fastest-reader.html.

Chapter 26

This Data Bank information comes from "the horse's mouth."

Speaker Mark Shepherd explains school assembly fees at http:// drumsongstory.com/post/school-assembly-fees-explained/.

Plan ahead for your high school classes. Why? Because 39 percent of participants surveyed said their high school experience influenced their careers. See the 2008 Careerbuilder.com survey, in Rachel Zupek, "Geek, Jock, or Class Clown?" CNN.com, "Living," June 18, 2008, http://www.cnn.com/2008/LIVING /worklife/06/18/cb.more.successful/.

Chapter 27

The average person who is scammed via the Internet loses $600. See the iC³ Internet Crime Complaint Center Annual Report at http://www.ic3.gov/media/annualreport/2012_IC3Report .pdf.

Only about one third of families have a filter to protect kids from bad images and other awful stuff that can be found online. Ask your mom or dad to check out filtering software like Safe Eyes, Net Nanny, or K9. Some of them are free. If your parents want more info about the Internet and its danger to you, they can call Focus on the Family at 1-800-A-FAMILY or write to us at:

Focus on the Family, 8605 Explorer Dr., Colorado Springs, CO
80920.

Some people stay off the Internet because they don't like what they
hear about the online world. What kinds of people are more
likely to use the Internet? Do more men or women log in? See
Pew Internet and American Life Surveys, March 2000–May
2013, "Internet Adoption: 1995–2013," Pew Research Center,
"Trend Data (Adults)," http://www.pewinternet.org/Trend
-Data-(Adults)/Internet-Adoption.aspx. Also see Kathryn
Kickuhr and Aaron Smith, "Digital Differences," Pew Internet,
April 13, 2012, http://www.pewinternet.org/Reports/2012
/Digital-differences/Main-Report/Internet-adoption-over-time
.aspx.

Chapter 28

Some of the first Spin Pops featured Power Rangers. Want to
know which ones are worth the most money? At your library,
check out the book *Spin Pop Interactive Candy Toys* (Schiffer
Publishing, 2002) by Marc Zak for the history of the candy.

There was a rumor that eating Pop Rocks and drinking soda could
cause your stomach to explode. That just isn't true! To find out
more trivia about Pop Rocks, visit the home page Pop Rocks,
http://www.pop-rocks.com/f-a-q/.

Want your mom to buy you a motion-activated candy dispenser?
Tell her that the "touchless operation reduces germ transfer."
The machine will make you healthier! If she doesn't like the

idea of your having access to candy, the machine also dispenses unsalted nuts. Visit The Sharper Image, http://www.sharper image.com/si/view/product/Motion-Activated-Candy-Dispenser -/201659?question=CANDY MACHINE.

Chapter 29

Americans also spend more on bicycle gear and trips than they do on airplane tickets and fees. Did you spend money on a bike this year? For more fascinating facts see The Outdoor Recreation Economy (Boulder, CO: Outdoor Industry Association, 2012), http://www.outdoorindustry.org/pdf/OIA_OutdoorRec EconomyReport2012.pdf.

Chapter 30

To take a "You Be the Bee" test to see what you know about bee dances, visit "Dances with Bees," *Tales from the Hive*, NOVA, airdate January 4, 2000, http://www.pbs.org/wgbh/nova/bees /dancesroun.html.